CURBING THE BOOM-BUST CYCLE: STABILIZING CAPITAL FLOWS TO EMERGING MARKETS

John Williamson

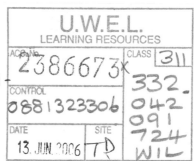
INSTITUTE FOR INTERNATIONAL ECONOMICS
Washington, DC
July 2005

John Williamson, senior fellow at the Institute for International Economics since 1981, was project director for the UN High-Level Panel on Financing for Development (the Zedillo Report) in 2001; on leave as chief economist for South Asia at the World Bank during 1996–99; economics professor at Pontificia Universidade Católica do Rio de Janeiro (1978–81), University of Warwick (1970–77), Massachusetts Institute of Technology (1967, 1980), University of York (1963–68), and Princeton University (1962–63); adviser to the International Monetary Fund (1972–74); and economic consultant to the UK Treasury (1968–70). Among his numerous studies on international monetary and developing world debt issues are *Dollar Adjustment: How Far? Against What?* (2004), *Dollar Overvaluation and the World Economy* (2003), *After the Washington Consensus: Restarting Growth and Reform in Latin America* (2003), *Delivering on Debt Relief: From IMF Gold to a New Aid Architecture* (2002), and *Exchange Rate Regimes for Emerging Markets: Reviving the Intermediate Option* (2000).

**INSTITUTE FOR
INTERNATIONAL ECONOMICS**
1750 Massachusetts Avenue, NW
Washington, DC 20036-1903
(202) 328-9000 FAX: (202) 659-3225
www.iie.com

C. Fred Bergsten, *Director*
Valerie Norville, *Director of Publications and Web Development*
Edward Tureen, *Director of Marketing*

Typesetting by BMWW
Printing by United Book Press, Inc.

Printed in the United States of America
07 06 05   5 4 3 2 1

Library of Congress Cataloging-in-Publication Data

Williamson, John.
    Curbing the boom-bust cycle: stabilizing capital flows to emerging markets / John Williamson.
        p. cm.
    Includes bibliographical references and index.
    ISBN 0-88132-330-6
    1. Capital movements—Developing countries. 2. Capital movements—East Asia. 3. Business cycles. 4. Financial crises. I. Title.

HG5993.W54 2005
332'.042'091724—dc22

2005043366

Contents

Figures

Boxes

Preface

One of the perennial problems with which the Institute has grappled over the years has been that posed by the debt of emerging-market countries. We have regarded it as natural and healthy for these countries to borrow from the international capital market, but we have also recognized that it is possible to have too much of a good thing. Both the Latin American debt crisis of the 1980s and the Asian crisis of the 1990s were outcomes of excess and posed many questions to us and other analysts. What strategy would preserve international financial stability and restore debtor country access to financial markets, and would this be consistent with renewed growth in debtor countries? Is it possible to design policy modifications that will reduce the chances of future crises developing? Is it possible to forecast future crises? How can the international community change its handling of crises that do occur so as to reduce their cost to both the debtor countries and the creditor financial community?

A theme explored by Donald Lessard and John Williamson in a 1985 study called *Financial Intermediation Beyond the Debt Crisis* was whether it would be possible to reduce the vulnerability of the system to crises by changing the instruments in which developing countries borrow. One of their suggestions was that financial markets develop the flow of portfolio equity capital, then in its infancy, to be a major source that would permit a permanent reduction in the role of bank loans. This book similarly examines the potential of new financial instruments, focusing in particular on growth-linked bonds and lending by multilateral development banks denominated in the borrower's own currency, as would be permitted by the MDBs themselves borrowing in a basket of indexed emerging-market currencies. The book also examines the potential role of other policies to reduce the vulnerability of the system and advocates such initiatives as the introduction of forward-looking provisioning by banks, retention of the ability to use capital controls in appropriate situations, and creation of a fiscal incentive to avoid currency mismatches.

The Institute for International Economics is a private, nonprofit institution for the study and discussion of international economic policy. Its purpose is to analyze important issues in that area and to develop and communicate practical new approaches for dealing with them. The Institute is completely nonpartisan.

The Institute is funded by a highly diversified group of philanthropic foundations, private corporations, and interested individuals. Major institutional grants are now being received from the William M. Keck, Jr. Foundation and the Starr Foundation. About 33 percent of the Institute's resources in our latest fiscal year were provided by contributors outside the United States, including about 16 percent from Japan. The Ford Foundation, the Rockefeller Brothers Fund, and the GE Fund provided support for this study.

The Institute's Board of Directors bears overall responsibilities for the Institute and gives general guidance and approval to its research program, including the identification of topics that are likely to become important over the medium run (one to three years) and that should be addressed by the Institute. The director, working closely with the staff and outside Advisory Committee, is responsible for the development of particular projects and makes the final decision to publish an individual study.

The Institute hopes that its studies and other activities will contribute to building a stronger foundation for international economic policy around the world. We invite readers of these publications to let us know how they think we can best accomplish this objective.

C. FRED BERGSTEN
Director
June 2005

Acknowledgments

This study has been a long time in the making, and accordingly it incorporates insights from many people whose roles may have been obscured by the mists of time. However, I know that I spent several days visiting the Bank for International Settlements in Basel and had some very fruitful discussions there at an early stage. Slightly later I visited New York, Boston, and Connecticut, and at different times also Frankfurt, London, Tokyo, and Zurich, in order to gain insights into how people in the financial sector viewed many of the issues. Colleagues and other participants in the Institute's several study groups on the topic contributed many helpful critiques. Singling out any one individual may be invidious, but I think Edwin M. Truman is the only person who read the entire manuscript twice in order to make sure that where I erred I was at least aware of the alternative viewpoint. I contributed papers that exploited some of the same material to the ASEAN Economic Associations Annual Meeting in Singapore in September 2000, published in *Monetary and Financial Management in Asia in the 21st Century*, Augustine Tan, ed. (Singapore: World Scientific, 2002), and to a WIDER Research Project, published in *From Capital Surges to Drought*, Ricardo Ffrench-Davis and Stephany Griffith-Jones, eds. (Basingstoke: Palgrave-Macmillan, 2003): On both occasions I benefited from very helpful feedback. I have also had the opportunity of discussing growth-linked bonds with their foremost proponents, notably Eduardo Borensztein, Kristin Forbes, and Paolo Mauro. And of course I have drawn on several generations of research assistants at the Institute for International Economics, most notably Jacob Kirkegaard and Kadee Russ, in putting together the quantitative information presented in the tables. I am grateful to everyone who contributed to the development of the analysis and ideas presented in this study.

Introduction

International investors poured vast sums of money into East Asian and Latin American countries during the mid-1990s, when the emerging-market boom was at its peak. Then Thailand stumbled, panic seized the markets, and boom gave way to bust. Investors suffered large financial losses. Asian countries suddenly experienced large capital outflows, and the macroeconomic pressures these wrought plunged countries that had been growing rapidly ("miraculously") into crisis. Much the same had happened in Latin America when the debt crisis broke in 1982: The banks that had lent money to the region suffered years of anxiety capped off by substantial losses, and the countries that had been growing nicely suddenly found themselves confronting a lost decade. Latin America again suffered a similar fate a few months after East Asia stumbled, in 1998. If one goes back in history, one finds that these are only the most recent of a succession of booms in lending to emerging markets that have given way to busts that impoverished both those who lent money and those who borrowed from them (Eichengreen and Lindert 1989).

That is not how the textbooks explain the consequences of capital mobility. The textbook picture is rather one of mutual gain, in which resources are shifted from areas of excess savings to areas with a surfeit of profitable investment opportunities or in which both parties benefit from portfolio diversification without any actual flow of real capital necessarily occurring. One can indeed think of cases where these gains were realized in practice: Canada's rapid development in the late 19th century with foreign capital, Norway's development of its oil industry in the 1970s, Singapore's success in growing by attracting multinationals, and Korea's heavy borrowing in the 1960s and 1970s.

Nevertheless, the outcome has all too often not been so benign. As Borensztein and Mauro (2004) recently summarized the historical survey in Bordo et al. (2001):

> External financing crises are far from being a novel feature of the international financial system: they have recurred at various times during the past two centuries, typically following periods of large financial flows . . . toward the emerging markets of the day.

The issue that is addressed in this study is whether it has to be this way or whether feasible policy actions could curb the sequence of boom and bust and thus permit both investors and emerging markets to tap the potential benefits of capital mobility without the costs of the crises that have so often ensued. That question is of particular importance at this time because many emerging markets seem to have reacted to the crises of the 1990s by ceasing to borrow, just at a time when demographics suggest that there is particular scope for gain by channeling Northern savings into investments in the South.

This study starts by analyzing the nature of the boom-bust cycle, first by looking at the general case and then by taking the East Asian case as an example of where lending went too far. It is argued that capital flows can be, and indeed frequently are, excessive. On the one hand, investors often act in herds and thus pour in foreign funds to a level that makes a crisis likely. On the other hand, borrowers have difficulty resisting the temptation to take all that is offered in the good times, are typically guilty of hubris ("this time it is different because . . ."), and end up taking too much. Crises are costly. In principle, one solution would be to cut the Gordian knot and end capital mobility (if one could), but that not only might be infeasible but (as analyzed in chapter 2) also would mean forgoing a series of real potential advantages that capital movements could bring.

A less drastic approach is to examine whether actions could be taken by creditors and debtors that might stabilize the flow of capital at a level that would make economic sense. As a prelude to this, chapter 4 examines the different forms of capital inflow, with a view to deciding which forms one might wish to promote at the expense of others as well as which forms are in particular need of action to reduce volatility. Chapter 5 contains a description of the asset management industry, that is, the institutional arrangements that govern many of those capital flows.

The two principal chapters of the book, chapters 6 and 7, are dedicated to examining the possibilities of action to reduce the volatility of capital flows on the part of the creditors and the debtors, respectively. So far as the creditors are concerned, the study identifies a series of relatively minor actions that could be helpful, but, unless—improbably—investors were to abandon their current focus on maximizing yields in each short-run period, the study concludes that capital flows would probably not be profoundly affected. Debtors could do more on their own account, but some of the actions that would seem most likely to be effective would require the agreement of the general international community, including the source countries, to change the international rules of the game. That is why cooperative international action will be necessary to achieve a significantly more stable flow of capital, with all the benefits that might entail.

It is the intention of this study to provide a guide to the set of actions that would seem most likely to further this outcome. No one should imagine that this will involve anything like complete stability in the flow of capital, but a significant diminution in the wild swings that have characterized the past seems both feasible and desirable.

2

The Problem of the Boom-Bust Cycle

The history of lending to emerging markets has not been happy. Mexico took its first foreign loan in 1824, three years after the consolidation of its independence in 1821, and first defaulted just three years later, in 1827 (Eichengreen and Lindert 1989, 142). Thereafter Mexico experienced long periods when it was frozen out of the international capital market as a punishment for having defaulted; these periods were followed eventually by debt reconstruction and the resumption of borrowing for a few years, until the next time the country encountered difficulty in servicing its sovereign debt. Matters have been similar in most other Latin American countries, with the Barings crisis in Argentina in the 1890s being the most famous upset before the Great Depression. Crises, defaults, and debt reconstructions were a regular part of history long before the 1980s debt crisis.

Indeed, Michael Bordo (1999) has shown that it was not the 1930s and the post-1980 periods that were the great historical exceptions to this pattern of crises, but the Bretton Woods years in between. The Bretton Woods years were the only lengthy period since the birth of capitalism in Holland in the 17th century that lacked major banking or debt crises. The Bretton Woods years were also, not coincidentally, the period when financial repression was practically ubiquitous. The end of that period was heralded by Carlos Diaz-Alejandro, who presciently titled a 1984 paper on the debt crisis, "Goodbye Financial Repression, Hello Financial Crash."

It does not follow that financial repression is a good thing, for by now a wealth of empirical evidence shows that allowing credit to be allocated by bankers who weigh expected return against risk results in a higher average rate of return (and therefore higher productivity and growth) than the alternative of allocation by bureaucrats. What it does suggest is that

Figure 2.1   Net inflows of foreign capital to developing countries, 1970–2003

billions of US dollars

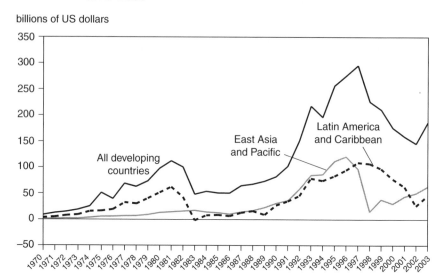

Note: Data for net inflows are provided in tables 4.1–4.3, column 10.

Source: World Bank, *Global Development Finance,* 2004.

the process of financial liberalization needs to be approached with a great deal of caution and with a lot of care to install an effective system of prudential supervision that will deter bankers from acting in the interests of their cronies rather than their ostensible principals, depositors, and shareholders. It will be argued later that one of the lasting impediments to capital mobility should take the form of rules designed to ensure that banks and other financial institutions conduct their international operations prudently.

Capital flows to developing countries were minimal throughout the Bretton Woods period. They began to build up in the early 1970s. Figure 2.1 shows the total level of net capital inflows to developing countries from 1970 to 2003 as well as the flows to each of the regions of more advanced emerging markets, namely East Asia and Latin America. Even allowing for the fact that dollar prices somewhat more than tripled from the early 1970s to the turn of the century, it can be seen that capital flows were on a strong upward trend during this period. The second thing that one notices is that the upward movement is superimposed on a strong cyclical pattern. From modest beginnings before 1974, the total exploded during the second half of the 1970s as commercial banks began recycling petrodollars primarily to Latin American middle-income developing countries. The total peaked in 1981 and then more than halved by the nadir of the Latin American debt crisis in 1983. Lending to Asia continued, and the total gradually climbed after 1986 as investors became enamored of the Asian miracle. By 1992, the nominal total surpassed the level of 1981. The next few years saw a renewed boom as Latin America came back to the markets in a big way in the early 1990s after the Brady Plan had dealt with the debt overhang and investors had recognized the profound policy changes in train. The year 1994 witnessed a mild decline in Latin America as a result of the tequila crisis, but lending to Asia continued to boom, and aggregate capital flows reached a new peak in 1997. The Asian crisis then brought a collapse that was reversed only in 2003, but 2003–04 again witnessed what looks to be the start of another boom. In short, capital flows to emerging markets have been nothing if not volatile.

Capital Flows as Drivers of Cycles in Emerging Markets

In recent years, the flow of foreign capital has become the prime driver of the business cycle in a number of emerging markets, especially in Latin America. That the process is driven primarily by variations in the availability of foreign capital rather than by developments in the host countries seems strongly indicated by the large size of the variations in the overall flow (as shown in figure 2.1). If capital flow variations were largely a reflection of differences in the attractiveness of the destination, one would expect to see little cyclical variation because the differences between one country and another would tend to cancel out. Neither can one dismiss the variations in flows as simply reflecting the business cycle in the developed countries, because these countries were not in recession throughout the debt crisis of the 1980s or the Asian crisis of the 1990s. It seems rather that, as José Antonio Ocampo (2003) has emphasized, the variations in capital flows are driven primarily by changes in risk evaluation. When foreign investors develop an appetite for risk (Ocampo points out that this should more properly be called an underestimation of risk), there is a boom in capital flows; the bust is marked by a flight to quality (risk aversion).

Why should investors' risk appetites change in this way? One factor that empirical work in the early 1990s (Calvo, Leiderman, and Reinhart 1993) showed to be of far greater importance than had previously been assumed is the state of liquidity in the markets of the developed countries. Investors flock to emerging markets when alternative investments appear unremunerative. This theory suggests that capital flows to emerging markets typically get under way early in the cycle and tend to tail off before the cyclical peak in the developed countries. Some economists have also continued to argue that evidence of economic reform in emerging markets acts as a pull factor that cannot be neglected. The bulk of the evidence, however, seems to point to a dominant role for push factors coming from the developed countries. The policy implication is that this provides yet one more reason for urging developed countries to do as much as possible to stabilize the cycle—and also to maximize the use of fiscal rather than monetary instruments to that end. And swings tend to get magnified by what George Soros calls the "principle of reflexivity," which implies that the fundamentals really are better when capital is readily available.

When foreign investors want to lend to an emerging market, the external interest rates at which the enterprises and government of that emerging market can borrow are relatively low, and available maturities tend to be long. This encourages spending, certainly by enterprises considering investment. It also makes it easy for governments to finance budget deficits, although whether they will fall for the temptation depends upon political economy. A government that tries to resist the boom by maintaining a restrictive fiscal stance, even if its resistance is only through allowing the automatic stabilizers to work, may find itself subjected to criticism for not exploiting the country's good fortune in the new era that is always perceived to have dawned.[1] When the boom ends and capital starts to flow out, interest rates will rise; this will further worsen the budget deficit and thus cause additional cutbacks in primary spending. The effects are stronger if the public debt is predominantly short term.

A central bank that tries to dampen the boom by maintaining a restrictive monetary policy will find that its high interest rates serve to accentuate the capital inflow. This has a cost to its bottom line if it sterilizes the inflow and a cost to its inflation-fighting credentials if it does not. Even if the central bank tries to sterilize the inflow, asset prices are likely to be driven up so that wealth owners find their net worth rising without the tedium of having to save. Similarly, the real exchange rate tends to appreciate so that everyone except exporters tends to feel wealthy. Conditions are in place for a boom. All this goes into reverse, with a vengeance, if and when there is a sudden stop to the capital inflows, let alone a net outflow.

Sudden stops certainly happen. The question that is usually asked is the extent to which they can be blamed on policy weaknesses in the capital-importing country rather than on an exogenous reduction in investors'

---

1. It has even been argued by Talvi and Vegh (2000) that optimal fiscal policy involves a pro-cyclical tax cut at such times; because the political pressures to spend the whole of a country's tax receipts are overwhelming, it is preferable to avoid having a surplus to spend. This is, in fact, a second-best argument conditional on the political irremovability of the propensity to spend everything combined with the postulate that public spending achieves less than the same value of private spending.

risk appetites. It is easy to identify weaknesses after a crisis has occurred: Any country that suffers a crisis is, for example, likely to experience a precipitate increase in its ratio of debt to GDP. In addition, some countries suffer capital flight, as Indonesia did after its exchange rate was set free to float in 1997.

Some crises are clearly initiated by the results of misguided policies, as when reserves erode in a country that is trying to maintain a relatively fixed exchange rate. A lot of theory was built on the notion that countries tended to guarantee their borrowings (either explicitly or implicitly, e.g., by fixing their exchange rates in terms of the dollar, which may have attracted investors to think of dollar borrowing as almost riskless) and, in that way, encouraged currency mismatches that made them vulnerable. But in other cases—Malaysia and Indonesia in 1997 were perhaps the clearest examples until little Uruguay got clobbered by the Argentineans, who, when they were unable to withdraw their bank deposits in Argentina in 2001, turned instead to their accounts in Montevideo—crises were initiated by contagion. None of this is to deny the motherhood-and-apple-pie observation that countries are less likely to get hit by crises if they follow disciplined macroeconomic and financial policies.

Excessive Capital Inflows

A number of countries—Chile, Colombia, Malaysia, and even Brazil and Thailand at one point—have come to believe in real time that the inflows they were experiencing were excessive; they have therefore tried to dampen them by imposing some form of restraint. What problems did they see in large inflows?

A first and major issue is the fear of catching "Dutch disease."[2] Some economists argue that a country should unreservedly welcome capital inflows because capital inflows provide more real resources and therefore permit more consumption or higher investment. Others (including myself) regard this as a case in which more is not necessarily better. The

---

2. Dutch disease derives its name from its initial diagnosis in the Netherlands in the early 1970s, after large-scale development of newly discovered reserves of natural gas. The resulting inflation and improvement in the balance of payments led to an appreciation of the real value of the Dutch guilder, which devastated the traditional tradable-goods industries, meaning manufacturing. This led to unemployment in the short run and a fear that the rundown in the technologically progressive part of the economy would jeopardize future growth in the long run. Nowadays, Dutch disease is used to refer to anything—a boom in exports of natural resources, a capital inflow, or even large sums of aid—that causes a large real appreciation and thus jeopardizes manufacturing and other employment-generating traded-goods industries. See Corden (2002) for discussion by an economist who takes a much less tragic view of the problem than I do.

argument is that there are pretty convincing reasons for believing that it is only the tiniest countries that can expect to thrive without a dynamic manufacturing sector because manufacturing offers possibilities of learning by doing and cumulative progress that are largely absent in most other sectors. It follows that a country can jeopardize its long-run prospects by allowing such a large real appreciation—the natural consequence of a large capital inflow—that it undercuts the ability of its manufacturing sector to compete in world markets.

This is not just a theoretical curiosum. In 1979, the time of the second oil shock, Indonesia and Nigeria had similar per capita incomes. Both experienced a large increase in oil receipts because of the sudden rise in the price of oil, but their macroeconomic policy reactions were diametrically different (even if their tolerance of corruption was uncomfortably similar). Indonesia devalued its currency to keep its nonoil exports competitive; Nigeria allowed its currency to become hopelessly overvalued and thus killed off its other export industries as well as any import-substituting industries that were not the beneficiaries of protection (Bevan, Collier, and Gunning 1999). This was perhaps the most important of the policy differences that enabled Indonesia to reduce poverty to a fraction of what it was 30 years ago (despite the 1997 crisis) as Nigeria stood still.

The importance of a competitive exchange rate in promoting exports and growth has recently been popularized in the writings of Dooley, Folkerts-Landau, and Garber (e.g., 2003), who have drawn a parallel between the Bretton Woods system and the actions of China and other East Asian countries in pegging their exchange rates to the dollar. As a historical analogy, the parallel is far-fetched because the Bretton Woods system included an obligation to adjust an exchange rate in the event of a fundamental disequilibrium, and the United States ran current account surpluses instead of deficits virtually throughout the period, but their papers have succeeded in propagating the notion that growth can be promoted by an undervalued exchange rate. This is an important half-truth, but it is only a half-truth. The serious critique of their analysis is that it ignores the traditional constraint on growth that was discussed in the preceding paragraph: the resource scarcity that normally constrains investment and, thus, growth.[3] A proper analysis (such as I attempted in Williamson 2003) factors in both the importance of a competitive exchange rate in stimulating the demand to invest and the availability of savings—which are diverted from the domestic economy by a current account surplus—with which to undertake the investment.

---

3. It can be argued that in China today the real constraint on growth comes not from investment but from absorptive capacity, but, even so, one should ask whether investing in US Treasury bills, with their likely negative return in terms of Chinese goods, rather than increasing consumption, is the way to maximize intertemporal welfare.

A second possible reason to be suspicious of excessive capital inflows is the fear that some inflows may "immiserize." The original analysis of immiserizing capital inflows was presented by Brecher and Diaz-Alejandro (1977), who showed that under standard neoclassical assumptions a country would be worse off if capital were attracted into its protected sector and received the full (untaxed) value of its marginal product. That case is of limited relevance today, given the trade liberalization that has occurred since 1977 and the presumption that foreign direct investment (FDI) usually brings spillover benefits with it. Some people, however, regard recent investment in the Chinese automobile industry as a possible example. Moreover, Ronald I. McKinnon and Hugh Pill (1999) argue that many of the same dangers arise when capital flows into ill-regulated financial sectors, especially if such capital receives implicit credit guarantees, since it can again lead to investment in projects that are socially uneconomic.

A third reason is that most models suggest that there is an optimum level of capital inflow and that a greater inflow will serve to decrease rather than increase welfare. For example, Liqing Zhang (2004) built a model in which the optimum level of capital inflow occurs when the marginal revenue of the capital inflow equals its marginal cost. The latter may remain unchanged over a wide range, but the former may be expected to decrease with the capital inflow because other productive factors (including institutional variables like effective macroeconomic management, sound corporate governance, and banking supervision as well as skilled labor and appropriate technology) are predetermined.

A fourth and overwhelmingly important reason for fearing excessive inflows arises from the role of inflows in promoting the boom-bust cycle. A forward-looking government should fear that at some unpredictable moment the inflows will go into reverse and capital will rush for the exits or, at the least, the new inflows will suddenly stop. This situation becomes more likely the larger the stock of foreign capital is (especially the stock of short-term foreign capital) relative to the means of servicing the debt, of which the conventional measures are reserves, exports, or GDP. Hence, a capital inflow that raises the ratio of short-term debt to reserves, or the ratios of debt to exports and debt to GDP, will make a country progressively more vulnerable to a run, especially if the country has a fixed exchange rate. The worst situation is to have a big foreign debt (relative to exports and GDP), of which a large part is in the form of short-term loans that can be quickly withdrawn without the investor suffering a financial penalty even if other investors are trying to do the same thing at the same time. It is when a country is unable to finance such an outflow that it has guaranteed to permit—which is what pegging the exchange rate amounts to—that it suffers a foreign exchange crisis.

Overborrowing and the East Asian Crisis

The East Asian crisis[4] started in Thailand in 1997 for fairly traditional reasons involving the attempt to hold a fixed exchange rate that had become overvalued in the face of a large balance of payments deficit and a large volume of short-term foreign debt. It was then transmitted to the other countries of Southeast Asia (especially Indonesia and Malaysia) by contagion. Korea's situation is less clear than Indonesia's and Malaysia's because it already had a domestically induced banking problem, but it is not obvious that this would have spilled over to a foreign exchange crisis in the absence of the ill-advised foreign borrowing of the preceding years and contagion from the crises in Southeast Asia.

These countries were vulnerable to contagion because they had large stocks of badly structured foreign debt accumulated in previous years as a result of the capital inflows. The debt was badly structured in that it involved too much debt relative to equity,[5] too much short-term debt relative to long-term debt, too much foreign currency debt relative to domestic currency debt, and too much borrowing from the same set of creditors. Both the policy of pegging the exchange rate, which encouraged currency mismatches, and the peculiarities of the corporate sector, which induced borrowing rather than the sale of equity, contributed to the bad debt structure. Some believe that implicit guarantees of bank deposits by the public sector were a major factor generating moral hazard that led to excessive debt, but this view seems difficult to square with the particular countries that fell victim to crisis (Thailand instead of Bangladesh, for example).

The main alternative to contagion in explaining the outbreak of the crisis is that it was provoked by crony capitalism and insufficient diligence in implementing free-market orthodoxy. No one doubts that crony capitalism and corruption were present in unhealthily large measure, but the key question is whether they had worsened in the years before the crisis. The International Monetary Fund (2003) asserts that such a worsening occurred through the 1990s in the case of Indonesia, but I am not aware of similar evidence that cronyism had worsened in the case of Malaysia. In the absence of any such demonstration, one has to ask why a crisis should

---

4. The large literature on the East Asian debt crisis includes an important study of the IMF's Independent Evaluation Office (IMF 2003) and a recent review article by me (Williamson 2004). Some earlier contributions are the project of the National Bureau of Economic Research (see www.nber.org/crisis), Radelet and Sachs (1998), Furman and Stiglitz (1998), Krugman (1998), and Berg (1999). The classic source has long been the Web site of Nouriel Roubini, www.stern.nyu.edu/-nroubini/asia/AsiaHomepage.html.

5. The *IMF Survey* of December 14, 1998, gave estimates of debt-equity ratios of more than 900 percent in Indonesia, about 500 percent in Korea, more than 400 percent in Thailand, and about 100 percent in Malaysia (which is about the level typical of industrial countries). IMF (2003) revised the estimate of the Indonesian debt-equity ratio down to a still high, though no longer astronomical, 250 percent.

Table 2.1   Corruption rankings and scores of selected Asian countries, 1996

Country	Ranking	Score
Singapore	7	8.80
Japan	17	7.05
Hong Kong SAR	18	7.01
Malaysia	26	5.32
South Korea	27	5.02
Taiwan	29	4.98
Thailand	37	3.33
Philippines	45	2.65
India	46	2.63
China	50	2.43
Bangladesh	51	2.29
Pakistan	53	1.00

SAR = special administrative region

Note: Countries are selected from a total of 54 countries ranked. A high ranking and a low score indicate a more corrupt country; a perfect score is 10, which indicates no corruption.

Source: TI Corruption Perception Index 1996, Transparency International, Berlin. www.transparency.org/cpi/1996/cpi1996.pdf.

suddenly have exploded when it had not done so during the many years before and when the economic performance of Malaysia, as of the other countries of the region, had been spectacularly good. The simple fact of the existence of crony capitalism does not build up a cumulatively larger danger, in the way that capital inflows do as a debt burden progressively accumulates.

It is in any event possible to examine whether the countries that succumbed to crisis were indeed particularly corrupt. Transparency International calculates and publishes each year a Corruption Perceptions Index for a large number of countries, based on foreign businesspeople's assessments of how much corruption they face in each country. The rankings for 1996 (the year preceding the crisis) are shown in table 2.1 for each of the 12 Asian countries among the 54 that were covered by the index that year (unfortunately Indonesia was not among them).

Everyone agrees that Indonesia, Malaysia, Korea, and Thailand were engulfed by the crisis. It has been conventional to include the Philippines as a fifth crisis country, but in Williamson (2004) I argue that, if one measures by the impact on GDP, one should include Hong Kong instead. In either event it can be seen that the crisis countries are at worst in the middle of the pack instead of being distinguished by a particularly high level of corruption. This is not surprising if one takes the view that the crisis was essentially caused by the countries borrowing too much, for it requires a certain minimal level of governance before the markets will be prepared

Table 2.2 Economic freedom rankings and scores of selected Asian countries, 1997

Country	Ranking	Score
Hong Kong SAR	1	1.25
Singapore	2	1.30
Taiwan	7	1.95
Japan	11	2.05
Thailand	23	2.35
South Korea	27	2.45
Sri Lanka	27	2.45
Malaysia	36	2.60
Philippines	50	2.80
Indonesia	59	2.85
Pakistan	78	3.10
Mongolia	93	3.35
Cambodia	106	3.55
Nepal	108	3.60
Bangladesh	118	3.70
India	118	3.70
China	125	3.80
Myanmar	140	4.30
Vietnam	143	4.70
Laos	148	5.00
North Korea	148	5.00

SAR = special administrative region
Note: These are the Asian countries among a total of 148 countries ranked. The scale goes from 1 (perfect economic freedom) to 5 (total economic repression).

Source: 1997 Index of Economic Freedom, Heritage Foundation, Washington.

to lend a country enough to get it into trouble. Counting Hong Kong among the crisis countries makes the countries that succumbed to crisis less rather than more corrupt than average.

As for the lack of free markets, perhaps the best measure we have of countries' performance in this regard is the Heritage Foundation's economic freedom index. Table 2.2 shows the 1997 rankings and scores of the 21 Asian countries that were covered by the index that year. (Those measures were assessed in 1996, before the crisis had a chance to influence perceptions.)

All the crisis countries come in the top half of table 2.2. Indeed, if one agrees with my contention that Hong Kong should be counted as a crisis country, the crisis countries become quite clearly the countries that enjoyed markedly above-average economic freedom. Even the lowest ranked country, Indonesia, ranked 59th out of 148 countries. These figures suggest that countries with free markets were more, not less, likely to get overwhelmed by the crisis. The reason is not difficult to fathom: One aspect of free markets is capital account convertibility, and it is this that made countries vulnerable to contagion and capital flight.[6] This is a far more convincing explanation than one that blames the East Asian crisis on crony capitalism or a lack of free-market orthodoxy.

Costs of Crises

Virtually no one benefited from the crises. Many investors lost a lot of money despite all the talk about bailouts and moral hazard: IMF loans saved the skins of some banks, but other banks and almost all equity investors suffered losses. Michael Barth and Xin Zhang (1999, 204) estimate that at one point foreign investors had lost something on the order of $166 billion during the crisis. Of course, this was not all permanent loss: Most asset prices recovered somewhat, and those investors who did not panic and sell out in the middle of the crisis benefited from that subsequent rebound. Nonetheless, the financial losses suffered by investors are not to be dismissed.

Far more serious, the countries that were victims of the crisis suffered severe recessions. This is not historically abnormal: Bordo et al. (2001, 28) summarize the historical experience of financial crises during the past 120 years as resulting in "downturns lasting on average 2 to 3 years and costing 5 to 10 percent of GDP." Table 2.3 shows three estimates of the growth that the East Asian countries at the center of the recent crisis forfeited as a result of the crisis. The top part of table 2.3 shows actual growth rates over 1991–2003. The bottom parts of the table show three estimates of the losses they suffered as a result of the crisis during the 1997–2000 period. The first block of the lower part shows how much GDP fell short of where it would have been had these countries maintained the average growth rates they achieved in the first half of the 1990s. The sums of these figures provide an estimate of the cumulative growth shortfall caused by the crisis. Below is a single column showing comparable estimates of cumulative lost GDP for the same four-year period, 1997–2000, made in a study by the Committee for Economic Development. The final block of columns shows similar calculations for three of the four crisis countries, plus the Philippines, using Centre d'Études Prospectives et d'Informations Internationales (CEPII) estimates of what potential growth rates would have been in the absence of the crisis instead of assuming that potential growth would have equaled actual growth rates in the earlier part of the decade.

It is obvious that the losses are staggering for all countries except the Philippines, which actually did somewhat better during the crisis period

---

6. One might also note that the poor scores of China, India, and Vietnam, the three fastest growing large countries in the world in the second half of the 1990s, cast doubt on the usefulness of this index as a predictor of future growth.

Table 2.3   Growth rates and growth gaps in East Asia, 1991–2003

Growth rates

Country	1991–95 (average)	1996	1997	1998	1999	2000	2001	2002	2003
Hong Kong SAR	5.6	4.3	5.1	−5.0	3.4	10.2	0.5	2.3	3.3
Indonesia	7.3	8.0	4.5	−13.1	0.8	4.9	3.5	3.7	4.1
South Korea	7.5	7.0	4.7	−6.9	9.5	8.5	3.8	7.0	3.1
Malaysia	9.5	10.0	7.3	−7.4	6.1	8.6	0.3	4.1	5.2
Thailand	8.5	5.9	−1.4	−10.5	4.4	4.8	2.1	5.4	6.7
Memorandum:									
Philippines	2.2	5.8	5.2	−0.6	3.4	4.4	3	4.4	4.5

Growth gaps

Lost GDP, cumulative (percentage of a year's GDP)	1997	1998	1999	2000	Total, 1997–2000
Hong Kong SAR	0.5	11.1	13.2	8.6	33.4
Indonesia	2.8	23.2	29.7	32.1	87.8
South Korea	2.8	17.1	15.1	14.0	49.0
Malaysia	2.2	19.0	22.4	23.2	66.8
Thailand	9.9	29.0	33.1	36.9	108.9
Memorandum:					
Philippines	−3.0	−0.2	−1.5	−3.7	−8.4

Lost GDP (percentage of a year's GDP)	Cumulative, 1997–2000
Indonesia	82
South Korea	27
Malaysia	39
Thailand	57

Lost GDP	Trend without crisis (middle scenario)	1997	1998	1999	2000	Total, 1997–2000
South Korea	7.1	2.4	16.4	14	12.6	45.4
Malaysia	6.5	−0.8	13.1	13.5	11.4	37.2
Thailand	6.4	7.8	24.7	26.7	28.3	87.5
Memorandum:						
Philippines	2.5	−2.7	0.4	−0.5	−2.4	−5.2

SAR = special administrative region

Sources: Growth rates: Berg (1999); IMF, *World Economic Outlook,* April 2004; Committee for Economic Development (2000, table 5); Berthelemy and Chauvin (2000).

Table 2.4 Indicators of collapse of Asian intermediaries and estimates of cost of bank recapitalization since 1997 Asian crisis

Indicator	Indonesia	Korea	Malaysia	Thailand	Philippines
Banks and finance companies[a] (percent)					
Closed or suspended	7.0	28.6	0.0	51.9	n.a.
Nationalized, administered by restructuring agency, or planning to merge	29.4	3.6	68.3	3.7	n.a.
Costs of bank recapitalization (percent of GDP)					
JPMorgan	20	30	20	30	0
Standard & Poor's	20+	20+	18	34	n.a.
Cost of bank restructuring (percent of GDP)					
IMF	32.5	19.5	19.3	35	4.5

n.a. = not available

a. Percentage based on number of firms affected as of April 1998 relative to firms existing in July 1997.

Sources: Statistics on affected intermediaries: *The Economist* (April 4, 1998); recapitalization costs: Berg (1999); restructuring costs: IMF (2003).

than its historical norm, which is why it is silly to count it as a crisis country. (Doubtless it, too, suffered pressures, as did other countries like Singapore, but its reactions—including the decision to take much of the strain by letting the exchange rate depreciate—sufficed to fend off the crisis.) For the other five countries, losses far exceeded the historical norm of 5 to 10 percent of GDP. With historical experience as the counterfactual, losses come to more than 80 percent of a year's output in Indonesia and Thailand and to sums between one-third and two-thirds of GDP in the other crisis countries. The CED and CEPII figures show only modestly smaller losses. Unless one believes that the East Asian miracle was in any event running out of steam and that growth would have been much slower than in the early 1990s even without the crisis, it seems that both Indonesia and Thailand lost over a half year's output and that the losses in all five of the crisis countries exceeded one-quarter of a year's output.

The currency crises were accompanied by banking crises in Indonesia, Korea, Malaysia, and Thailand. Estimates of the costs of recapitalizing the banking systems of these countries are shown in table 2.4. These costs largely involve recognition of costs that were imposed on society by bad lending during the preceding boom, although depreciation and recession added to the number of loans that turned bad and in that way accentuated the costs. Some economists will argue that these costs are only transfer payments, not real costs like the loss of GDP that results from a recession. That is true, but it does not mean that these large payments have no wel-

Table 2.5 Impact of East Asian crisis on unemployment, 1990–2003
(percent)

Country	1990–95 (average)	1996	1997	1998	1999	2000	2001	2002	2003	Job losses, 1998 (thousands)
Indonesia	3.7	4.9	4.7	5.5	6.4	6.1	8.1	9.1	n.a.	2,944
South Korea	2.4	2.0	2.6	6.8	6.3	4.1	3.7	3.3	3.4	1,222
Malaysia	3.6	2.5	2.6	3.2	3.4	3.1	3.7	3.5	3.6	162
Thailand	1.7	1.1	0.9	4.4	4.2	3.6	3.3	2.4	2.2	805
Memorandum:										
Philippines	8.6	7.4	7.9	9.6	9.6	10.1	9.8	10.2	10.1	362

n.a. = not available

Source: Asia Recovery Information Center database.

fare significance. An interesting paper by Diwan (1999) established that the share of labor in national income usually falls sharply following a financial or banking crisis. Although it recovers subsequently, the recovery is typically only partial. A natural interpretation of Diwan's stylized facts is that the bill for recapitalizing the banking system is paid largely by immobile factors of production, meaning, in practice, unskilled labor. For anyone who worries about income distribution, the cost of recapitalizing the banking system should certainly be a matter of concern.

One reason that it is right to be concerned about economic losses is because of the human costs they impose. The East Asian crisis resulted in increases in unemployment (table 2.5), which were sharp at least in South Korea and Thailand. The increase shown for Indonesia looks extremely modest, indeed implausibly so, inasmuch as the figure given by the same source for the number of job losses in 1998 suggests that the increase in unemployment must have been much larger. Moreover, in most cases the victims lacked unemployment compensation. The crisis interrupted and at least temporarily reversed the decline in poverty that had been the crowning achievement of the East Asian miracle (table 2.6): At least 10 million people (one World Bank estimate was as high as 20 million) were pushed back below the World Bank's extremely modest dollar-a-day absolute poverty line. Fortunately the impact on the social statistics appears to have been rather less brutal than that on poverty; for example, infant mortality only edged up (and Thailand avoided even that), but before the crisis it had been declining each year.

Crises and Progress

It would only be if crises were inseparable from progress that one could look at such statistics without concluding that it would make sense to try to attenuate the cycle of boom and bust. There are indeed economists who

Table 2.6 Impact of East Asian crisis on social indicators in East Asia, 1990–2002

Social indicator	1990	1996	1997	1998	1999	2000	2001	2002
Population living under national poverty line (percent)								
Indonesia	20.6	7.8	n.a.	n.a.	12	10.5	8.9	7.5
South Korea	n.a.	9.6	n.a.	19.2	n.a.	n.a.	n.a.	n.a.
Thailand	12.5	2.2	n.a.	3.9	4.3	3.7	3.2	2.6
Philippines	19.1	14.8	12.1	14.5	13.0	12.0	11.3	11.0
Population living on less than $1 per day (millions)								
Indonesia	39.6	15.5	n.a.	n.a.	24.9	22.1	19.0	16.3
Thailand	7.3	1.3	n.a.	2.4	2.7	2.3	2.0	1.6
Philippines	n.a.	10.4	8.7	10.6	9.7	9.2	8.8	8.7
Infant mortality rate (per 1,000 live births)								
Indonesia	63	49	47	48	48	44	42	40
South Korea	12	9	9	10	22	10	8	7
Malaysia	15	11	11	11	11	11	7	6
Thailand	38	34	33	29	29	22	18	21
Philippines	44	37	35	35	36	33	31	29

n.a. = not available

Source: Database, Asia Recovery Information Center.

believe that crises are the inevitable price of progress, and they attribute this view to Schumpeter (creative destruction). A somewhat less extreme view is that of Ranciere, Tornell, and Westermann (2005), who argue that financial liberalization tends to both increase growth (by facilitating risky investment) and induce crises. If a crisis at the end of several decades of vigorous growth is the price to be paid for the preceding growth, it might be a bargain, but the question is whether it is plausible to suppose that growth is promoted by policies that also give rise to crises. The evidence that domestic financial liberalization leads to faster growth (at the cost of a greater likelihood of crises) is persuasive, but the evidence that a liberalized capital account accelerates growth is thin (see chapter 3). In contrast, the evidence that an open capital account makes a country more vulnerable to crises is overwhelming.

An alternative view is that it is perfectly possible to combine the dynamism of a market economy with a reasonable measure of macroeconomic stability and an absence of financial crises. It is, after all, possible to argue that macroeconomic stability encourages investment and innovation rather than that stability precludes investment and innovation. The weak entrepreneurs and dumb ideas that some of Schumpeter's disciples argue are weeded out by a stock market decline and the accompanying recession can perfectly well be eliminated by investors figuring that the present value of a particular enterprise is negative without the whole market having to collapse. Indeed, the panic associated with a general market collapse runs the danger of wiping out worthwhile companies along with the rubbish. Financial supervision is intended to reconcile decentralized decisions on credit allocation that will result in high productivity of the loans and, therefore, high growth with prudence that will minimize the chances of crises developing. Capital can be channeled to enterprises and regions enjoying high returns without allowing booms to get out of hand. Indeed, it is when capital flows into countries experiencing asset price booms that it is most prone to be wasted.

How can one decide whether booms followed by crises are the inevitable price of progress or whether a fierce boom-bust cycle actually impedes progress? Ask yourself whether you believe that one of the factors underlying the East Asian investment boom was the region's macroeconomic stability preceding the mid-1990s or whether, on the contrary, you believe that the boom of the mid-1990s was just what was needed to cap off the miracle. Ask whether there were dot-coms that went bust while the NASDAQ was booming, or whether its bust was necessary to weed out the junk. Consider whether you believe that all the companies that went under during the Great Depression were either run by weak entrepreneurs or were pursuing dumb ideas. Recall that the investors who fed the speculative booms in East Asia and New York lost a lot of money, and ask whether you think they were the agents responsible for emergence of the New Economy.

Anyone who agrees with my answers to those rhetorical questions will also agree that progress is best fostered by creating a microeconomic environment in which those who innovate can be confident of retaining the fruits of their initiative, within a stable macroeconomic environment. No one should imagine that this is going to entail perfect macroeconomic stability without any business cycle, but there is a world of difference between the wild oscillations that so many emerging markets have suffered in recent years and the rather gentle cycle that the industrial countries have become accustomed to. The objective is to tame the boom-bust cycle of the emerging markets to make it something closer to the genteel fluctuations of the rich world. Obviously other things are involved in creating growth besides establishing property rights and macroeconomic stability—for example, providing good technical education in which potential innovators will get the training to be able to figure out what innovations are worth making and how to make them—but the point is that there is little reason to suppose that the environment will be improved by a sequence of booms and busts rather than by a measure of stability. That is why it is worth asking whether and how it might be possible to curb the boom-bust cycle.

3

The Case for Capital Mobility

If capital account crises are indeed the threat that was suggested in chapter 2, why not resolve them by simply prohibiting capital flows? Why not cut the Gordian knot?

The answer is twofold. One reason is that we have no instrument sharp enough to stop capital flows. Capital controls leak. That does not render controls completely ineffective, as the evidence of significant premia in the presence of controls demonstrates (Cooper 1999). But it does force one to recognize that complete control is simply not feasible as well as pose the question as to whether it makes sense to risk corruption by trying to impose controls.

The other and more positive reason for not attempting to proscribe capital flows is that capital mobility brings benefits as well as costs. This chapter is about those benefits.

Reallocating Capital

The classic benefit of international capital mobility is that it provides the ability to divorce the level of investment within a country from the level of national savings. Countries with relatively large investment opportunities at the world rate of interest, compared with their national savings, can borrow from abroad; high-savings countries (relative to investment opportunities) can in turn lend. Both parties expect to gain, just as in other voluntary economic transactions: The capital exporter gains because it earns more than it could do by investing at home, while the capital importer gains because the extra investment it is enabled to undertake earns more than it has to pay. As Eichengreen and Mussa (1998, 12) put it:

> Flows from capital-abundant to capital-scarce countries raise welfare in the sending and receiving countries alike on the assumption that the marginal product of capital is higher in the latter than the former. Free capital movements thus permit a more efficient allocation of savings and direct resources toward their most productive uses.

Note that achieving these gains is inherently dependent on current account imbalances. It is necessary to have a deficit in the borrowing country and a surplus in the lending country in order to transfer real capital from the lender to the borrower. As the debt comes to be serviced, this current account imbalance will be reversed.

It is this factor that underlies the presumption that emerging markets ought normally to be capital importers and industrial countries ought normally to be capital exporters. Emerging markets are short of capital relative to their supply of labor and natural resources; hence, the yield on capital ought to be high, according to standard neoclassical theory. Industrial countries are capital rich; hence, the standard presumption is that the yield on capital will be low. Both gain if capital is redeployed from areas of relative plenty to those of relative scarcity, where its yield is higher. The traditional view of how this works over time in a typical country, based on the neoclassical model that offers the same production function to all countries, is summarized in the model of the debt cycle (see box 3.1).

It has been recognized for some time that this model generates predictions about the magnitude of the differentials in rates of return to capital and the size of capital flows that are dramatically larger than observed in reality (Lucas 1990). How does one explain this, and does it suggest that one should reject the whole notion that welfare gains are likely if capital flows from capital-rich to capital-poor countries?

A possible answer is suggested by the school of thought that has recently questioned the magnitude of the benefits to be expected from the convergence in capital/output ratios permitted by capital mobility. Gourinchas and Jeanne (2004) constructed and calibrated a neoclassical model (or rather two models, a Ramsey-Cass-Koopmans model with just physical capital and a "Macro-Mincer" model that also incorporated human capital accumulation) to examine the magnitude of the gains from financial integration. They found that these were typically small compared with other sources of gain. For example, the gain from a switch from complete financial autarky to perfect capital mobility might be of the order of a 1 percent increase in permanent consumption even for a country whose initial capital stock doubled as a result of financial integration. The most important reason for the modest impact is the essentially transitory nature of the distortion introduced by capital controls: With the assumption that the natural rate of interest is the same among countries, over time a country will accu-

Box 3.1   The debt cycle

The notion that the basic purpose of capital flows is to redistribute capital to the countries where the productivity of capital is highest has been elaborated into the theory of the debt cycle. The basic assumptions made in this analysis are that technology is the same in all countries, that there are diminishing returns to capital, and that the propensity to save is constant over time.

Consider the situation in a poor country when it is first integrated into the world economy. It will have a low capital-labor ratio and, hence, a high marginal return on capital at the level of investment that can be financed by the limited flow of domestic savings. The country therefore has an incentive to borrow abroad, which means that over time it will build up both its capital stock and its foreign debt.

The higher capital stock enables output to increase. A part of this is diverted into servicing the external debt. In due course the debt service comes to exceed the capital inflow, and the resource transfer (which is defined as capital flow minus debt service payments) becomes negative. This is the second stage of the debt cycle. An unthrifty country (one with a low saving propensity) will settle down into a steady state in this stage. It will have higher output, income, and consumption than it would have had without capital mobility, but its net resource transfer will be negative.

A thrifty country, in contrast, will move on through a series of three further stages. In the first of these—the third stage of the debt cycle—it will start to generate domestic saving greater than its domestic investment requirements, even after servicing its foreign debt. The excess saving will be lent abroad, increasing the negative resource transfer but starting to decrease the external debt.

The fourth stage of the debt cycle starts when the country has repaid its entire (net) external debt, and it becomes a creditor country. At that point it starts to receive net interest income from abroad, although the resource transfer remains negative because the capital outflow continues and exceeds the receipts of interest income.

The fifth and normally the final stage of the debt cycle occurs when external assets have accumulated to the point that the interest they yield exceeds the capital outflow. This is the "mature creditor country," which enjoys a positive resource transfer even as it plows back a part of its foreign investment income into new investment and, therefore, sees its foreign assets continue to grow. This is also a possible steady-state position and will indeed be the one realized by a thrifty country, with a current account surplus equal to a part of its interest income just large enough to support a rate of foreign asset accumulation equal to the growth rate of the domestic economy. This is where Britain and France were before World War I.

A pathological sixth stage is possible in a country when its propensity to save decreases. This could lead a mature creditor country to start living off its foreign capital, consuming not merely its interest income but importing capital as well. This is not a possible steady state; it leads in due course back to stage one, where the United States has been in recent years, and then on to stage two.

mulate the capital for itself, and the benefit from financial integration will wither away. The long-run level of output is unaffected, and some part of the short-run growth acceleration accrues to the foreign investors.

The principal reasons for international welfare differences are to be found in different levels of distortion and productivity, according to Gourinchas and Jeanne, and, unless capital account opening alters these, the process of financial integration will not have a large impact. This accords with recent growth literature, where the previous emphasis on factor accumulation as the principal source of growth (embodied inter alia in the Lucas paper cited above) has been superseded by the view that differences in total factor productivity account for most income differences across countries.

While this interesting analysis should induce a certain element of caution in arguing that there are large potential gains from capital mobility, it would be premature to dismiss the classical source of gains as inherently trivial. Apart from the fact that some of the cross-country empirical studies suggest a more substantial effect (on which more below), one should note two theoretical points.

One, the underlying model is not the traditional neoclassical model in which the same technology is available to all countries; it is instead the endogenous growth model in which it is the growth rate of labor-augmenting productivity rather than the level of per capita output that converges across countries. I, at least, have never felt comfortable with the assumptions of a common natural rate of productivity increase while productivity levels are country specific and exogenous to the capital flow. These assumptions exclude both the traditional neoclassical model and a Lewis-type model of growth, in which people are transferred from a low-productivity subsistence sector to a modern sector in a process that requires investment in order to raise total factor productivity.

Two, the natural rate of interest (the rate of interest when the economy is in steady state) is the same across countries. This assumes that all countries have the same rate of time preference (as well as natural rate of productivity increase). If consumers are more (or less) impatient in one country, there would be scope for that country to raise its welfare by borrowing from (or lending to) the rest of the world in steady state.

Hence, I will not dismiss the possibility that a substantial flow of capital from capital-abundant to capital-scarce countries could be a significant factor in accelerating growth in those that are capital scarce. Indeed, a case can be made that capital flows motivated by a search for the highest productivity of capital ought to offer substantial welfare gains in the coming decades, even greater than those portrayed by the debt-cycle model. The industrial countries face the problem of an aging population, but at present they have unusually large cohorts in the preretirement, high-savings phase of the life cycle, which is roughly between the ages of 45 and 64. It has been estimated that this effect could raise aggregate savings in the Organization for Economic Cooperation and Development (OECD) countries from something greater than $1 trillion in 1990 to approximately $1.4 trillion in 2010 (World Bank 1997, 116).

The populations of these countries are also fairly stagnant or in some countries even declining in total size, implying limited investment needs. One would therefore expect them to have both an ability to save more than they invest and a motivation for investing the surplus in emerging markets so as to earn debt service that can support pension payments as the retired proportion of the population increases in the future. This will enable them to finance spending in excess of the income generated at home as the ratio of retirees to the working population increases.

At the same time, a large part of the developing world should be at the stage of development where returns on capital are unusually high. Nowadays it is generally believed that this time of high returns on capital is not in fact the primitive stage of minimal capital accumulation as under the neoclassical assumptions of the debt-cycle model, but it occurs instead after a country has developed the basic human and institutional infrastructure needed to permit catch-up growth. Many emerging markets— most of Asia and Latin America—are now in this situation, and optimists hope that the laggards in Africa and elsewhere will also achieve takeoff in the next decade or two. Almost all of these countries are also either already well along toward or, at the latest, starting the demographic transition, where birth rates fall progressively so as to ease and ultimately end population growth. At this stage, the largest age cohorts in these countries either are entering, will soon enter, or have recently entered the working population, which suggests that they will be able to absorb large volumes of capital in productive investment with a high rate of return at the same time that industrial countries have surplus savings to invest.

The pattern of capital flows suggested by this analysis of demographic-development potential is from the industrialized countries to the more advanced of the developing countries, the emerging markets, and such a pattern of international capital flows did indeed prevail during the 1990s, up until the Asian crisis. Since then there has been a reversal, with the United States, which was already a capital importer, increasing its borrowing to a point at which it outweighs the net lending of the other developed countries, while East Asia, the part of the developing world that seems to best match the description of a natural capital importer, has become a capital-exporting region. For a time, one could hope that this was a temporary aberration caused by East Asia's need to rebuild its liquidity position following the crisis rather than a permanent shift in the pattern of capital flows, but so far it has shown no sign of ending even though East Asian countries have now rebuilt their reserves to levels that look more than adequate.[1]

Admittedly, there is a school of thought that sees the emergence of current account surpluses in the East Asian countries as a manifestation of a new development strategy, export-led growth, instead of as a perverse capital flow that threatens growth (see, for example, Dooley, Folkerts-Landau, and Garber 2003). I find this view unpersuasive. It assumes that

---

1. Even the cautious IMF concluded that ". . . the rapid buildup of foreign exchange reserves in some emerging markets . . . may now be approaching the point at which some slowdown in the rate of accumulation is desirable." (IMF, *World Economic Outlook 2003*, 91).

growth is always and everywhere constrained by a shortage of demand, and it neglects the need for adequate supply capacity. The other consideration that needs to be factored into analysis is that supply can be limited by a shortage of capital if excessive real resources are absorbed in a current account surplus.

A correct analysis of export-led growth recognizes both the importance of a competitive exchange rate for generating foreign demand and the cost of an excessively competitive exchange rate in diverting real resources into low-yield investment in foreign assets. The growth-maximizing exchange rate is that where these two effects are equal at the margin (Williamson 2003). This view recognizes that several East Asian countries (Indonesia, Malaysia, and Thailand) were already pursuing a successful policy of export-led growth before the crisis of 1997 even though they had current account deficits. Their export successes had made them attractive locations in which to invest, and the capital inflow financed their current account deficits. (Thailand—at least—overdid it, which is why a crisis occurred.)

Nor is this analysis fatally undermined if one believes that in some surplus countries—China comes to mind—growth is constrained by absorptive capacity, not investment. Absorption can be increased by stimulating consumption rather than investment. If one believes, as I do, that the yield on dollars added to Chinese reserves in terms of Chinese goods will certainly be negative, then even with a zero rate of time preference, Chinese intertemporal utility would be increased by additional consumption and a smaller current account surplus.

It should therefore be an important objective of policy to secure a resumption of flows from capital-rich to capital-poor parts of the world. Since 2002, a major pickup has been occurring in the flow of private capital into emerging markets, but at present this is offset by their reserve buildups, reinforced to some extent by a net reduction in the stock of official lending and an outflow of resident capital. Their current account balances remain decisively in surplus (collectively to the tune of more than $100 billion per year). A part of the international adjustment process to reduce the US current account deficit to a sustainable level needs to be an expansion of domestic demand in the emerging markets and a consequential reduction or elimination of their collective current account surplus. This would be potentially beneficial to both parties—the United States and the emerging markets.

Not only would a reversion to the more normal pattern of net capital flows from industrial countries to emerging markets help raise global growth prospects, provided it were financed appropriately, but it would also help relieve the pressure for large flows of migrants into the industrial countries with aging populations and rising ratios of retirees to workers. This is not to suggest that any likely level of capital flows either should or will eliminate such migrant flows, which seem bound to be substantial unless current demographic trends change sharply. Nevertheless, the greater the capital inflows that help developing countries raise their living standards, the less will be the differential in income levels and opportunities that drives migrants to seek better lives outside their native countries. Whether this shows up in fewer immigrants whose large-scale absorption raises social problems to both communities (however much we might wish it were otherwise) or in less-Draconian measures to try to prevent illegal immigration, the consequence will be an unambiguous gain in human welfare.

Consumption Smoothing

A second way in which capital flows can raise economic welfare is by permitting a smoother path for consumption, given the path of output through time. This happens when a country hit by a negative shock (such as a bad harvest or low prices for its commodity exports) is able to borrow and then repay out of the proceeds of a positive shock (a particularly good harvest or high commodity prices) at some later time. Conversely, a country that enjoys a positive shock should be able to build up its stock of foreign assets and then run them down again to sustain consumption when confronted by a negative shock. Calculations reported in Prasad et al. (2003, appendices 3 and 4) imply that the potential gains from this source for developing countries are large, especially in the case of small economies.

Experience suggests that developed countries are able to achieve these gains of consumption smoothing, but this is a lot more difficult for developing countries, even for the more advanced ones that are now called emerging markets (see, for example, Gavin, Hausmann, and Leiderman 1995). Developing countries can save and build up their foreign assets in response to a positive shock if their authorities can resist the political temptation to splurge. It may later be difficult, however, to persuade the markets to view a subsequent rundown of the assets as prudent, in which case the objective of smoothing consumption will be thwarted. Certainly it is difficult to persuade the markets to increase their exposure to an emerging-market country that has been hit by a negative shock, even when the country was not overindebted to begin with. Chile's decade-long capital inflow dried up in 1998 when the price of its copper exports dove as a result of the Asian crisis, precisely when it actually needed capital inflows—which in preceding years had been so abundant as to constitute an embarrassment—in order to sustain activity. Prasad et al. (2003) concluded that the volatility of consumption growth increased relative to volatility of income growth in emerging markets in the 1990s, the decade in which financial globalization increased, suggesting that consumption volatility was aggravated, not diminished, by opening the capital account.

Regrettably, it is therefore unrealistic to include consumption smoothing among the major gains from capital mobility that can be expected by emerging markets in the near future. Matters might change if capital markets were to shake off the short-termism that currently afflicts them, but that is something on which it would be unwise to count in advance of evidence that it has occurred.

Risk Diversification

A third source of welfare gain from international capital movements may be as important as the first: risk diversification. Because risks are less correlated between countries than within countries, an investor can expect to be exposed to less risk to achieve a given expected rate of return (or to achieve a higher rate of return for the same level of risk) by holding an internationally diversified portfolio. This factor is of particular potential significance to residents of small, undiversified economies, whose wealth is otherwise highly dependent on the fortunes of their country's main export products.

Not only does the possibility of risk diversification benefit individuals directly because of less variability in their income streams, but it can also have an indirect benefit in terms of allowing investment to be channeled into more productive avenues. With limited diversification possibilities, prudent investors will not be prepared to invest large sums in high-yield, high-risk projects. As the pool of investors becomes larger and more diverse, so does the possibility that some of them will find it prudent to invest parts of their portfolios in more risky projects that will on average yield higher returns. Hence the average yield of investment can be expected to rise as well.[2]

Note that these welfare gains from diversification do not necessarily depend on current account imbalances at the time when the investment occurs. It is in principle possible for investment flows in opposite directions to exactly offset each other, but this is quite consistent with both parties gaining *ex ante* from the transactions.

One thinks of risk diversification as being an important motivation for portfolio investment by institutional investors such as pension funds and insurance companies as well as for capital outflows from developing countries. Such flows may well contribute to reallocating capital as well. Two important papers of Henry (2000a, 2000b) have shown that portfolio equity has major effects in terms of stimulating the level of investment. On the basis of an empirical examination of 12 countries that liberalized international access to their equity markets in the early 1990s, Henry finds

---

2. Maurice Obstfeld (1994) argued, on the basis of a theoretical model that he attempted to calibrate with stylized data, that this factor is quantitatively important.

that on average they experienced abnormal increases in stock prices approaching a cumulative 30 percent over a period of some eight months leading up to liberalization. One would expect this reduction in the cost of capital to stimulate investment, and Henry found that this indeed happened. On average the countries experienced a temporary investment boom of about three years' duration, during which private investment increased by some 22 percentage points more than would have been expected otherwise.[3] This result contrasts with the traditional macroeconomic literature, which has concluded that capital inflows other than foreign direct investment (FDI) and aid tend to be split between consumption and investment in much the same proportion as domestic income.[4]

Nevertheless, it is also important to recognize the possibility that capital mobility without any net flow of capital can lead to important welfare gains. Contrast, for example, a situation in which the pension funds of an emerging market are restricted to domestic investments in the home market, a small monocrop economy that also excludes foreign portfolio equity investment, with one in which an outward flow of pension fund money is offset by foreign investments in portfolio equity. The capital stock, and therefore GDP, will be identical in the two cases. What would differ would be the volatility of pensioners' incomes, which would oscillate with the fortunes of the monocrop in the first case and be smoothed by investment in a world portfolio in the second case. This is not a case of smoothing pensioners' incomes at the expense of the rest of the population; international investment would bring with it less volatility in national income as well.

In practice, one should expect that during the next several decades the flow of money into emerging markets from pension funds of the industrial countries will exceed the outward flow of money from pension funds established in emerging markets. Industrial countries' pension funds are already nearer maturity, so that the switch of a small portion of their portfolios into emerging markets will provide a flood of money, while pension funds in most emerging markets are still small and undeveloped. As they grow, the disparity will gradually dwindle, so that eventually there may be rough balance between inward and outward placements. For the next several decades, however, portfolio flows are likely to bring benefits from the reallocation of capital as well as from portfolio diversification.

---

3. Another paper that investigates the impact of liberalizing foreign investment in the equity market is Bekaert, Harvey, and Lundblad (2001). They reached similar conclusions to Henry. The summary in Prasad et al. (2003, box 1) mentions several other studies where the association between growth and portfolio equity inflows was found to be positive, but in most of these it was statistically insignificant.

4. One might ask how the traditional result can hold if portfolio equity, which is one of the constituents of the capital inflow other than FDI, in fact has a major effect in terms of stimulating investment. I suspect the resolution of this paradox is that the empirical studies underlying the traditional result were mainly based on data from times when capital flows were dominated by inflows of bank loans, not portfolio equity.

Access to Intellectual Property

A fourth distinct source of potential welfare gain from international capital movements arises when the flow takes the form of FDI. FDI normally brings with it access to intellectual property rights of some sort or another: patents, copyrights, technological know-how, managerial expertise, access to foreign markets, or a number of these factors. Stephen Hymer (1960) first pointed out many years ago that it is difficult to imagine why a firm should go to all the difficulties and dangers of operating in a foreign market if it did not have some advantage that would enable it to outcompete local firms, which have a greater familiarity with local circumstances. It is the chance to exploit its intellectual property rights in an extra market that typically makes investment attractive to a foreign firm.

Exploitation of these intellectual property rights normally brings spillover benefits to the host economy. The multinational enterprise pays taxes. It may pay wages higher than the prevailing rate, perhaps to buy itself standing as a good corporate citizen, and will in any event add to the demand for labor. It may increase competition in the national market, although this need not necessarily occur if it acquires a local firm rather than makes a greenfield investment. It often provides a conduit to the continuous upgrading of best practices over time.

FDI may enable a country to engage in completely new kinds of activities (production of semiconductors in Costa Rica or disk drives in Thailand). A multinational enterprise may also try to upgrade the technical standards of its local suppliers in order to protect its quality reputation in the international market. Managers or workers who learn skills on the job may move on in due course to local firms. A multinational enterprise may also carve out market share in the local market by supplying improved goods that were not previously available. A firm with better access to intellectual property can benefit its host economy via so many channels that one seems fairly safe in assuming that such benefits will materialize.

Unfortunately, there seems no very convincing basis for quantifying how large the benefits may be. Estimates are that the profit rate of multinationals averages some 14 percent while the stock of FDI is estimated at about $1.4 trillion, which suggests that multinationals' profits are approximately $200 billion a year. If they succeed in appropriating about half of their net contribution to the economies in which they invest, they are adding to the GDP of the host emerging markets some $400 billion (twice the $200 billion profit), half of which is earned by foreigners. The other half yields a net benefit to the host economy in the form of higher GNP.

A particular form of FDI consists of entry into the financial-services industry by foreign banks. These banks can and often do bring substantial benefits to the host economy in the forms of both a modernization of financial techniques and increased competition in the financial-services industry. Nowadays foreign banks tend to organize their lending in emerging markets through local banks that they have bought, and they finance this lending by taking domestic deposits rather than making international loans. This practice has the great advantage of avoiding exposing the borrower to currency risk, although it also means that the emerging market does not get an inflow of foreign currency.

One host-country worry about the presence of foreign banks is that the knowledge base of the local supervisory authorities may be undermined by the fact that many operations are beyond their purview (Committee on the Global Financial System 2004). Another potential problem exists: If the domestic banks are in a parlous financial situation, the intensification of competition may push them over the brink into "gambling for resurrection." The moral is that, when it is opening its financial sector, a country needs to be careful that either the domestic financial system is financially sound or that a strong regulatory setup is in place that is capable of restraining imprudent lending. Obviously it is better if both are true.

FDI can in principle be financed internally, by borrowing. But in practice it usually involves a substantial measure of external financing: The 2000 *World Investment Report* (UNCTAD, *World Investment Report 2000*, 19) concluded that approximately 70 percent of FDI was financed by an inflow of equity capital (plus another 10 percent or so by retained earnings). FDI is therefore normally (though not inevitably) associated with a capital inflow and, hence, with the possibility of financing a larger current account deficit. Empirical evidence (UNCTAD, *World Investment Report 1999*, 172) suggests that FDI inflows are typically translated entirely, or perhaps even more than entirely, into increased investment. That points to another spillover benefit of FDI: It generally appears to stimulate local investment rather than displace it.

Prasad et al. (2003, box 1) summarize evidence of the effect of different forms of capital inflow on growth. The one form of capital inflow that appears to have a strong and robust positive association with growth is FDI.

Discipline

Another advantage sometimes claimed for foreign borrowing is that it subjects the borrowing country to the discipline of the international capital market. For years the Indonesians used to tell themselves that one of the great advantages of their early adoption of capital account convertibility was that this restrained them from adopting populist or nationalistic policies that would not pass muster with international financiers. Nowadays Thomas Friedman eulogizes the "electronic herd"; his fantasy (Friedman 1999, 94) of how Robert Rubin might have responded to Mahathir Mohamad after his speech at the IMF/World Bank annual meetings in Hong Kong in 1997 includes:

The herd knows only its own rules. But [these] rules . . . are pretty consistent—they're the rules of the Golden Straitjacket. . . . It makes snap judgments about whether you are living by those rules, and it rewards most lavishly those countries that are transparent about what they are doing. The herd hates surprises. For years Malaysia seemed to be living by those rules. . . . But when you started to break the rules by overborrowing and then overbuilding, well, the herd sold you out. . . . [W]hen that happens you don't ask the herd for mercy, you don't denounce the herd as a "Jewish conspiracy," you just get up, dust yourself off, put your Golden Straitjacket on a little tighter and get back with the flow of the herd. Sure, this is unfair. In some ways the herd lured you into this problem: It kept offering you all this cheap money and you took it and overbuilt. . . . The herd is not infallible. . . . It overreacts and it overshoots. But if your fundamentals are basically sound, the herd will eventually recognize this and come back.

Friedman is right about the proclivity of the market to lure countries into borrowing too much, about the overreaction and the overshooting. He may also be right in thinking that the market will sooner or later return if the fundamentals are sound. But asking one to accept this sort of arbitrary discipline as a benefit of capital mobility is going too far; it might be more reasonable to count it as a cost rather than a benefit. Doubtless the fear of losing capital has sometimes been a stimulus to more responsible macroeconomic or financial policies (e.g., the primary surpluses in Brazil and Turkey), but as long as the markets swing wildly from euphoria to an absolute refusal to lend—which, it may be noted, does not seem to occur in developed countries—it is difficult to see a net benefit here.

Evaluation

Even if it were possible to prevent capital from moving internationally, this analysis suggests that one would not want to try. International capital flows offer the prospect of major welfare benefits. There is no need for facile analogies to trade in goods ("economists know that free trade in goods is beneficial, so free trade in capital must be too") in order to make the case that capital mobility has the potential to advantage both lender and borrower.

Capital mobility may also bring costs. Once upon a time people used to worry about foreign control of domestic industry, and nowadays the antiglobalization folks are concerned about the homogenization resulting from the same multinational enterprises selling the same goods everywhere. Opponents of globalization also appear to harbor suspicions that multinationals use the implied threat to move elsewhere to keep wages low, although it is difficult to see how this could result in wages lower than they would have been without the presence of the multinational. In fact, empirical evidence seems to suggest that, at least by host-country standards, multinationals generally pay relatively high wages (Moran

1998, 62). A full accounting of cost, however, needs to include that imposed by the boom-and-bust cycle and the repeated crises examined in chapter 2. Is there any evidence that can hint at how that cost compares with the benefits?

The obvious approach is to examine whether there is evidence of net benefits accruing from an open capital account. A number of studies have sought evidence as to whether an open capital account increases a country's income. Three of the early empirical studies (Alesina, Grilli, and Milesi-Ferretti 1994; Kraay 1998; and Rodrik 1998) failed to detect any benefit from overall capital account liberalization in terms of the promotion of a faster rate of growth, while one (Quinn 1997) found a positive impact from the liberalization of capital flows. Are these findings in conflict, or is it possible to reconcile them?

Kraay's measure of capital account openness was the total flow of capital (inflows plus outflows) as a share of GDP, which is quite distinct from the other authors' attempts to measure what the rules say. No attempt is made to reconcile Kraay's finding, but the conflicting conclusions of the other three authors may be due to an important difference in their specification of capital account openness. The two studies that found no impact tried to measure whether the capital account was open or closed,[5] whereas Quinn sought to construct a measure of the degree to which the capital account was open (using data from the IMF's annual report on Exchange Arrangements and Exchange Restrictions).[6]

Most countries liberalized FDI relatively early on, and most also liberalized long-term capital before short-term capital. As argued above, we have strong reasons for believing that liberalization of FDI should be beneficial for growth; there is also evidence that is somewhat less overwhelming, but still pretty convincing, that portfolio equity brings benefits. It is also reasonable to suppose that long-term (patient) capital will be beneficial. It is what is usually the last stage—opening up to unlimited flows of short-term money—that is problematic. Thus, many of Quinn's observations were presumably drawn from episodes where there was a strong probability that the net benefits of greater liberalization were positive; it is therefore not surprising that he found a positive effect. In contrast, the test of Alesina, Grilli, and Milesi-Ferretti and Rodrik was whether complete liberalization is beneficial, and both found no evidence that it is.

---

5. Rodrik took the proportion of years in which the capital account was free of restrictions, but the test was whether the capital account was completely free of restrictions.

6. A second but less crucial difference concerns the sample of countries: 20 OECD countries in the case of Alesina, Grilli, and Milesi-Ferretti; a mixed panel of 64 developing and industrial countries in the case of Quinn; and a large panel of exclusively developing countries in the case of Rodrik.

If one assumes that all three studies are basically right, the implication is that one should not try to please the New York investment banks by totally liberalizing capital flows, including the short-term froth the electronic herd likes to play with, but that there are real benefits from liberalizing FDI, portfolio equity, and long-term bonds and loans.

An important paper on this topic is Edison et al. (2002). They examined five measures of international financial integration (IFI), using three different econometric procedures to try and find a relationship between IFI and growth. Their work controlled for the standard determinants of growth, notably initial income, initial schooling, and macroeconomic balance. They also searched to see whether IFI had a positive impact on growth if certain conditions were satisfied—high per capita GDP, high educational attainment, a high level of financial-sector development, a high level of institutional development (good law and order and low government corruption), low inflation or high fiscal surplus. Their results were almost uniformly negative. They stated (766) that their results "suggest the lack of a robust relationship between IFI and economic growth." Nor did they find statistical evidence supporting any of the theories that IFI has a positive impact on growth provided that some critical condition (high per capita income, or financial development, or whatever) were satisfied. Note, however, that all five of their measures of IFI related to total capital flows or stocks rather than to the particular forms of capital flow—FDI, portfolio equity, and long-term bonds and loans—identified above as presumptively beneficial, so that the interpretation previously offered is not refuted by Edison et al.

An influential recent paper that surveyed and summarized the state of the art is Prasad et al. (2003), some of whose results have already been mentioned. Summarizing the results of 14 papers (including the 5 mentioned above), they comment (31) that "the majority of the papers [11 out of 14, actually] tend to find no effect or a mixed effect [of financial integration on growth] for developing countries. This suggests that, if financial integration has a positive effect on growth, it is probably not strong or robust." In seeking to explain a result that presumably offended their priors, they resorted to the same explanation as Gourinchas and Jeanne (2004): that the major source of cross-country differences in per capita income is to be found in differences in total factor productivity rather than the ratios of capital to labor that could in principle be equalized by capital mobility. They also acknowledge (34) another possible explanation: that some developing countries have experienced costly banking crises in the process of financial integration, which neutralized the benefits of greater capital inflows. The fact that greater financial integration—unlike trade opening—does not bring with it clear benefits is rubbed home by a fascinating demonstration that lower trade barriers are associated not just with faster growth but also with greater longevity and lower infant mortality, while greater financial integration fails to bring either health or growth benefits.

The view of the new growth theorists that per capita income primarily reflects differences in total factor productivity, not different capital-labor ratios, has introduced an element of doubt about the magnitude of the benefits of capital mobility. Nevertheless, this doubt about the magnitude—which is still a conjecture rather than a certainty, at least for those of us who doubt whether total factor productivity rises independently of the volume of investment—does not throw into question the notion that capital mobility has a number of very real advantages. It would thus be foolish to try to break the boom-bust cycle by closing the capital account, even if that were feasible. The objective should be to make the flow of capital less unstable, not end it. Greater stability of the flow may not be consistent with complete capital account convertibility, and restrictions may impose a price in terms of some reduction in the average size of flow, insofar as controls on the movement of short-term capital deter some potential investors from investing at all. A balance between volume and stability is much preferable to either a denial of a need for a tradeoff or a corner solution.

4

Forms of Capital Flow

Chapter 3 implies that countries need to be concerned about the form in which they borrow, perhaps even more concerned than with the level of borrowing. This chapter is devoted to taking a more detailed look at issues concerning the composition of capital flows and begins by developing a taxonomy of alternative forms of capital flow. It then takes a detailed look at the statistical facts about recent capital flows, seeking in particular to illuminate which of them are responsible for the boom-bust pattern. This is followed by an examination of the characteristics of the alternatives in terms of cost, conditionality, risk bearing, access to intellectual property, impact on investment, and vulnerability to capital flow reversal.

A Taxonomy

Capital flows can be categorized in a number of ways: by the direction in which capital flows, including by the type of lender or borrower, by the legal form of the contract governing the flow, and by maturity. Because the principal interest of this study is in countries that neoclassical theory leads one to expect to be capital importers, we will focus first and mainly on capital flows into countries, delaying a brief consideration of capital outflows until the end.

A first distinction is in terms of the type of lender.[1] The possibilities are

- foreign governments;

---

1. For convenience, purchasers of equity claims will be included under the term "lenders."

- multilateral development banks (MDBs), among which one may include the IMF for present purposes;[2]

- foreign nonfinancial corporations (which are important in this context mainly as sources of FDI but also in providing, or arranging for, supplier credits to finance sales of the capital goods they produce);

- foreign banks;

- other foreign financial institutions (pension funds, insurance companies, mutual funds, investment banks, and hedge funds, the latter two sometimes grouped under the label "highly leveraged institutions" despite the fact that they are not always highly leveraged);

- foreign individuals; and

- foreign nongovernmental organizations (NGOs).

A similar array of possibilities exists on the borrowing side, except that there is no equivalent to MDBs, unless national development banks are counted separately rather than as a part of the public sector. However, loans to individuals and NGOs are quantitatively unimportant.

In terms of the legal form of the contract, the possibilities are a grant; a loan; or an equity stake with control, which is FDI, or without control, which is portfolio equity investment.[3]

Maturity (or "tenor," as the financial people tend to call it) can vary from overnight (important in the interbank market) to infinite (as used to be the case with British consols and still applies to an equity stake, although either can be sold so that the individual investor is not permanently locked in).

A similar taxonomy is possible with regard to capital outflows from developing countries. The main difference is that there is again no analogy to MDBs among the sources of finance.[4] However, MDBs should be included among the foreign borrowers to whom residents may lend money.

---

2. Although the IMF has traditionally resisted being classified as an MDB, its Poverty Reduction and Growth Facility provides medium-term development finance.

3. It is a matter for debate as to how large an equity stake is needed to give control and, thus, to justify the label FDI. Clearly 51 percent is sufficient, but effective control is often possible with a much smaller stake. The conventional (arbitrary) dividing line is 10 percent, at least in the United States.

4. This statement again needs qualification. Some oil-exporting countries created joint or even national institutions (e.g., the Arab Fund for Economic Development, the Kuwait Fund) to lend government funds to poorer developing countries during the era of oil surpluses in the 1970s. Also, a number of developing countries subscribe to some multilateral initiatives; for example, 44 developing countries, including ones as poor as Bangladesh, subscribe funds to the IMF's Poverty Reduction and Growth Facility and its Heavily Indebted Poor Countries Initiative.

The Facts

Table 4.1 presents estimates of capital flows to developing countries from 1970, when private flows were in their infancy, to 2003. Data are shown for East Asia and Latin America in tables 4.2 and 4.3 to supplement those for the total of all developing countries in table 4.1. Box 4.1 provides descriptions of the data variables.

The decomposition given is based on that of the World Bank in its *Global Development Finance* (the successor to the *World Debt Tables*). It starts with equity flows, broken into FDI and portfolio equity (columns 1 and 2). In the early 1970s, FDI was the predominant source of private capital flows to developing countries, with Latin America then being a much bigger destination than East Asia. FDI then rose on a rather gradual trend through the 1970s and stagnated in total through the first half of the 1980s, with a continuing rise in East Asia more or less offsetting a decline in Latin America. A veritable explosion, presumably associated with the more welcoming stance of most developing countries, started in both regions in the late 1980s. Portfolio equity flows were modest in size until they also started to explode in the late 1980s.[5]

Columns 3 and 4 of tables 4.1 to 4.3 show bank loans with a maturity of more than one year, broken down between those made to public-sector and private-sector borrowers. One sees here the explosion in bank lending to sovereign borrowers in the 1970s following the oil crisis ("recycling petrodollars"), the cutback in the 1980s following the outbreak of the debt crisis (although with a delay in the cutback to the public sector as a result of the banks being arm-twisted into providing "new money"), and the explosion of bank lending to the private sector in the 1990s, followed by a new collapse after the Asian crisis.

Bond lending (columns 5 and 6) remained a minor element through the 1970s and 1980s, with no lending to the private sector recorded until 1989. Since 1993, private-sector to public-sector lending has been dominated by bonds, although in most years until the Asian crisis bond lending to the private sector was comparable with that to the public-sector borrowers. However, bank lending to the private sector grew even more than bond placements by the private sector, so that until after the Asian crisis there was no sign that banks were being disintermediated in the international context, as happened within financially developed countries like the United States.

---

5. When these flows were in their infancy, Donald Lessard and I (Lessard and Williamson 1985) identified portfolio equity as the most promising of a number of new channels that we explored for reviving capital flows to developing countries in the wake of the debt crisis. We were roundly criticized for being wildly optimistic in suggesting (in our table 9) that by the late 1980s portfolio equity could be yielding an annual flow of as much as $1 to $2 billion to all developing countries!

Table 4.1   Capital inflows and resource transfers for all developing countries, 1970–2003 (millions of dollars)

Year	FDI (net) (1)	Portfolio equity (2)	Bank loans Public sector (3)	Bank loans Private sector (4)	Bonds Public sector (5)	Bonds Private sector (6)	Other public sector debt Official creditors (7)	Other public sector debt Private creditors (8)	Short-term debt (9)	Total net inflows (10)
1970	2,062	−2	683	1,678	6	0	3,290	1,108	52	8,877
1971	2,620	−3	1,228	1,896	94	0	4,629	753	1,378	12,595
1972	2,325	−1	2,472	3,108	235	0	3,779	1,406	1,724	15,048
1973	3,554	1	4,711	2,197	131	0	4,738	1,278	2,201	18,811
1974	734	−3	6,076	5,875	119	0	7,362	1,862	3,258	25,283
1975	8,385	−5	9,307	4,857	225	0	11,488	3,453	13,498	51,208
1976	3,981	−1	11,250	3,865	1,050	0	9,456	4,594	5,351	39,546
1977	6,448	2	12,262	5,527	2,619	0	11,869	4,732	25,242	68,701
1978	8,130	1	17,200	5,565	3,416	0	12,864	5,685	10,112	62,973
1979	7,493	−1	25,404	7,249	1,105	0	14,418	5,413	12,347	73,428
1980	6,279	−1	19,571	9,216	1,123	0	20,473	11,641	29,501	97,803
1981	20,376	130	21,239	18,721	1,358	0	23,992	7,811	18,200	111,827
1982	23,050	−4	22,823	5,707	4,868	0	25,554	8,518	9,863	100,379
1983	14,999	−1	17,413	451	936	0	24,315	7,168	−17,068	48,213
1984	14,384	−2	19,936	−998	−433	0	22,209	6,374	−7,673	53,797
1985	12,274	46	7,076	−1,742	3,792	0	21,727	6,410	1,086	50,669
1986	10,904	225	7,844	−2,017	771	0	22,314	6,351	3,997	50,389
1987	9,394	282	12,958	−1,940	−341	0	23,053	7,181	14,071	64,658
1988	17,654	719	12,055	−2,905	3,145	0	19,367	6,724	11,006	67,765
1989	21,312	3,291	635	409	3,105	47	21,997	7,246	15,254	73,296
1990	24,032	3,004	−6,532	9,751	785	291	26,390	12,361	11,705	81,787
1991	33,106	6,541	−2,417	6,783	6,621	1,626	27,752	3,541	18,285	101,838
1992	45,399	12,991	2,709	12,629	1,247	7,350	23,029	11,167	34,860	151,381
1993	68,060	42,444	2,174	2,538	15,046	17,938	23,957	10,928	34,501	217,586
1994	89,894	35,810	−2,083	9,670	14,714	14,178	14,591	5,037	14,324	196,135
1995	105,303	17,320	7,626	20,869	13,319	10,092	22,347	1,815	58,343	257,034
1996	127,598	32,884	1,251	29,453	31,614	17,868	2,872	1,568	30,784	275,892
1997	171,095	22,594	7,068	36,838	19,121	19,097	9,776	2,046	7,986	295,621
1998	175,563	6,586	11,669	40,703	29,546	10,197	20,134	−5,090	−63,632	225,676
1999	181,722	12,640	−8,373	3,307	27,785	2,035	15,907	−2,323	−22,320	210,380
2000	162,170	12,633	−5,647	−174	19,698	−3,215	4,752	−5,463	−9,123	175,631
2001	175,035	4,397	−12,576	2,380	12,135	69	7,422	−7,270	−22,851	158,741
2002	147,086	4,945	−7,050	3,142	13,898	−1,159	−9,907	−7,031	1,435	145,359
2003	135,200	14,340	−5,782	−830	19,410	13,703	−14,310	−7,869	32,005	185,867

n.a. = not available

Source: See box 4.1.

Column 7 shows official lending, which naturally goes overwhelmingly to the public sector. This grew strongly through the 1970s, with the World Bank in a strong expansion phase under Robert S. McNamara's presidency and because bilateral foreign aid in the form of loans was still growing. Since then official lending has stagnated or even declined (al-

	Resident outflows			Interest payments				Interest received from abroad	Net resource transfer
Grants (11)	Bank deposits (12)	Portfolio investment (13)	Total (14)	Long-term (15)	Short-term (16)	IMF charges (17)	Earnings on FDI (18)	(19)	(20)
1,838	n.a.	n.a.	n.a.	2,289	1	0	662	60	n.a.
2,153	n.a.	n.a.	n.a.	2,543	0	0	1,232	56	n.a.
2,735	n.a.	n.a.	n.a.	2,962	0	0	724	59	n.a.
3,633	n.a.	n.a.	n.a.	4,127	0	0	2,978	115	n.a.
5,673	n.a.	n.a.	n.a.	5,857	0	33	4,460	150	n.a.
6,369	n.a.	n.a.	n.a.	7,370	78	114	4,685	120	n.a.
5,626	n.a.	n.a.	n.a.	8,134	200	228	6,453	121	n.a.
6,135	n.a.	n.a.	n.a.	10,074	895	296	10,470	97	n.a.
8,459	n.a.	n.a.	n.a.	14,307	1,699	303	11,098	143	n.a.
10,527	n.a.	n.a.	n.a.	21,166	3,060	304	10,459	308	n.a.
12,821	n.a.	n.a.	n.a.	30,633	13,904	454	17,890	273	n.a.
11,424	n.a.	n.a.	n.a.	37,930	18,965	658	24,500	227	n.a.
10,644	49,070	158	49,228	44,634	18,578	1,279	20,539	310	−22,924
10,130	18,480	−136	18,344	43,555	15,705	1,785	14,896	268	−35,674
12,341	2,160	29	2,189	49,502	13,285	2,678	14,051	466	−15,101
13,436	23,950	−383	23,567	51,504	12,547	2,840	12,909	448	−38,814
15,736	16,150	49	16,199	49,229	9,764	3,004	10,643	449	−22,265
16,714	23,450	−121	23,329	50,379	8,903	2,519	11,451	598	−14,610
18,086	6,720	7	6,727	57,990	10,628	2,271	13,081	490	−4,353
18,982	35,490	615	36,105	52,551	12,315	2,383	15,800	855	−26,020
27,737	37,010	−814	36,196	51,523	11,323	2,500	17,175	1,614	−7,579
33,928	−15,240	66	−15,174	51,985	13,257	2,494	18,277	2,150	67,078
30,104	−16,000	1,268	−14,732	50,892	10,737	2,439	20,571	2,506	114,085
27,669	−8,472	3,757	−4,715	48,993	12,635	2,343	25,456	3,316	163,858
31,700	19,798	2,269	22,067	57,039	14,082	1,804	31,266	2,980	104,557
31,590	1,794	9,227	11,021	73,033	16,604	2,788	43,708	5,285	146,753
26,799	4,494	8,470	12,964	76,704	18,068	2,309	48,454	6,876	151,068
25,290	11,999	20,125	32,124	82,006	19,028	2,207	56,333	8,913	138,127
26,719	5,306	6,018	11,324	90,745	17,602	2,502	57,318	8,607	81,511
28,519	24,747	36,613	61,360	95,732	16,606	2,843	59,185	8,964	12,136
28,705	9,189	10,373	19,562	101,001	17,891	2,881	76,556	10,857	−2,697
27,899	8,476	19,352	27,828	101,753	12,863	2,671	79,105	11,337	−26,243
31,228	−3,923	13,000	9,077	83,756	9,513	2,971	76,121	11,239	6,387
34,342	11,786	31,530	43,316	83,972	9,075	2,053	73,000	11,757	20,551

though the increase of grants has partially compensated at times). Column 8 shows lending to public-sector borrowers by private-sector lenders other than banks or via bonds: This consists largely of supplier credits and export credits provided by banks with a guarantee from an export credit agency. This tended to decrease in importance even before the Asian crisis, and since that crisis it has turned consistently negative.

Table 4.2 Capital inflows and resource transfer: Developing Asia Pacific
(millions of US dollars)

Year	FDI (net) (1)	Portfolio equity (2)	Bank loans Public sector (3)	Bank loans Private sector (4)	Bonds Public sector (5)	Bonds Private sector (6)	Other public sector debt Official creditors (7)	Other public sector debt Private creditors (8)	Short-term debt (9)	Total net inflows (10)
1970	201	0	48	380	−32	0	467	44	0	1,107
1971	283	−1	104	352	−7	0	414	119	232	1,497
1972	386	−1	240	466	12	0	662	252	247	2,264
1973	336	1	163	295	29	0	718	224	183	1,949
1974	729	−1	321	996	21	0	791	319	454	3,630
1975	1,032	−2	1,516	971	19	0	1,001	308	641	5,486
1976	969	1	708	787	336	0	1,344	796	947	5,888
1977	999	1	219	762	157	0	1,536	733	2,289	6,696
1978	991	0	692	163	422	0	1,668	785	2,232	6,953
1979	920	−4	2,311	564	244	0	2,161	898	2,088	9,181
1980	1,312	−4	2,572	1,030	194	0	2,384	2,025	3,380	12,894
1981	2,266	−1	2,438	1,620	52	0	3,629	1,141	3,321	14,467
1982	2,403	−1	3,311	1,533	1,043	0	3,462	1,405	2,512	15,667
1983	2,820	−1	2,631	1,481	1,766	0	4,393	1,832	2,244	17,167
1984	2,837	−1	1,446	1,067	276	0	4,833	1,320	2,204	13,982
1985	2,948	43	−1,005	329	3,267	0	3,413	2,387	1,259	12,641
1986	3,116	30	2,443	−114	1,574	0	3,144	577	−627	10,142
1987	3,912	201	3,408	266	874	0	4,367	−439	1,633	14,222
1988	6,738	486	1,977	910	−45	0	4,619	−38	2,363	17,010
1989	8,330	2,543	449	2,716	−38	31	6,360	972	1,456	22,818
1990	10,512	439	−1,305	7,152	−1,072	120	5,847	1,333	7,795	30,822
1991	13,192	−628	−461	6,035	128	410	6,777	1,355	9,447	36,257
1992	21,402	3,917	1,253	6,573	−445	720	7,060	5,565	11,620	57,667
1993	38,900	15,232	1,917	7	2,069	2,791	8,144	3,342	12,320	84,722
1994	45,562	9,404	180	2,832	3,654	5,729	5,677	3,310	9,732	86,081
1995	50,798	6,279	3,405	5,082	2,595	5,611	9,316	1,043	27,221	111,348
1996	58,638	9,664	−36	11,095	4,637	8,630	3,691	4,668	19,622	120,609
1997	62,138	−3,917	1,664	2,313	4,401	8,908	11,314	5,652	4,662	97,135
1998	57,662	−3,449	2,494	−7,285	1,314	−663	7,668	339	−43,341	14,737
1999	49,950	2,321	−3,461	−7,914	2,475	−1,588	10,666	−378	−13,879	38,194
2000	44,236	4,768	−4,832	−6,792	2,329	−3,975	5,750	−1,298	−10,127	30,058
2001	48,205	1,020	−4,310	−6,581	3,188	−2,514	5,723	−1,781	729	43,678
2002	54,834	3,493	−3,335	−6,051	3,052	−2,254	−5,123	−2,215	7,704	50,104
2003	56,800	4,800	−2,328	−2,604	4,961	850	−8,386	−3,540	12,061	62,613

n.a. = not available

Source: See box 4.1.

Column 9 shows short-term debt of all sorts, including trade credits, bank loans of less than one year to both the public and private sectors, and foreign purchases of treasury bills and commercial bills. One is immediately struck by the volatility of this series, which is even more striking in light of the fact that one of the main components, namely trade

	Resident outflows			Interest payments				Interest received from abroad	Net resource transfer
Grants (11)	Bank deposits (12)	Portfolio investment (13)	Total (14)	Long-term (15)	Short-term (16)	IMF charges (17)	Earnings on FDI (18)	(19)	(20)
624	n.a.	n.a.	n.a.	162	0	0	0	0	n.a.
718	n.a.	n.a.	n.a.	218	0	0	0	0	n.a.
941	n.a.	n.a.	n.a.	280	0	0	0	0	n.a.
859	n.a.	n.a.	n.a.	367	0	0	0	0	n.a.
1,083	n.a.	n.a.	n.a.	501	0	5	486	0	n.a.
854	n.a.	n.a.	n.a.	677	0	6	398	0	n.a.
712	n.a.	n.a.	n.a.	964	0	20	586	0	n.a.
740	n.a.	n.a.	n.a.	1,189	190	32	937	0	n.a.
987	n.a.	n.a.	n.a.	1,478	389	41	1,114	0	n.a.
1,117	n.a.	n.a.	n.a.	2,351	450	52	1,478	0	n.a.
1,131	n.a.	n.a.	n.a.	3,000	1,754	60	1,675	0	n.a.
1,041	n.a.	n.a.	n.a.	4,141	2,256	100	5,466	0	n.a.
919	6,330	169	6,499	4,642	2,605	190	5,325	0	−2,675
1,000	4,310	−80	4,230	4,942	2,191	200	5,256	0	1,347
1,262	−1,790	−1	−1,791	5,975	2,306	210	4,412	0	4,133
1,129	3,670	−208	3,462	6,143	2,229	187	3,694	114	−1,832
1,852	420	−43	377	6,753	1,560	173	2,652	86	564
1,948	2,310	−9	2,301	7,839	1,737	227	2,930	121	1,258
2,051	1,170	−17	1,153	8,969	1,778	226	3,365	119	3,689
2,186	4,700	643	5,343	10,082	2,202	250	4,342	153	2,939
2,081	4,250	−606	3,644	10,155	2,110	245	5,159	190	11,781
1,951	−1,000	36	−964	11,104	2,735	156	5,465	203	19,913
2,159	−2,160	0	−2,160	10,884	2,579	94	6,892	367	41,904
2,081	−2,200	−38	−2,238	11,574	2,808	127	7,166	709	68,075
2,730	2,800	0	2,800	13,064	3,658	73	7,286	732	62,661
3,081	587	0	587	15,542	5,015	69	17,709	997	76,503
2,333	1,451	0	1,451	16,263	5,672	41	20,576	1,330	80,269
2,356	2,611	0	2,611	17,860	6,903	51	22,722	1,138	50,482
2,460	2,801	1	2,802	19,024	5,041	361	22,681	404	−32,308
2,508	4,722	−153	4,569	20,219	3,841	565	25,799	1,046	−13,244
2,497	2,730	584	3,314	20,352	3,807	793	32,216	1,987	−25,938
2,164	1,666	2,303	3,969	18,658	3,375	692	32,419	1,247	−12,025
2,199	1,658	1,179	2,837	14,432	3,079	360	28,443	1,815	4,966
2,605	4,279	2,261	6,540	13,565	3,096	129	27,400	1,525	16,013

credits, is believed to be rather stable. Short-term loans turned strongly negative during the Asian crisis and remained in negative territory up to 2002. The volatility was confirmed by the strong bounce-back in 2003.

Total net capital inflows are shown in column 10. This figure gives a very partial picture of the extent to which the countries are importing real resources from the rest of the world in order to be able to increase absorption (investment or consumption). In the first place, capital inflows

Table 4.3 Capital inflows and resource transfer: Latin America and Caribbean (millions of US dollars)

Year	FDI (net) (1)	Portfolio equity (2)	Bank loans Public sector (3)	Bank loans Private sector (4)	Bonds Public sector (5)	Bonds Private sector (6)	Other public sector debt Official creditors (7)	Other public sector debt Private creditors (8)	Short-term debt (9)	Total net inflows (10)
1970	1,173	0	612	989	55	0	830	513	0	4,172
1971	1,665	0	904	1,121	117	0	700	269	658	5,434
1972	1,017	0	1,866	2,100	199	0	976	853	1,112	8,123
1973	2,329	0	3,173	1,145	74	0	1,175	620	1,143	9,659
1974	1,632	0	5,265	4,217	120	0	2,149	537	2,040	15,959
1975	3,370	0	5,679	3,039	151	0	2,662	366	1,574	16,841
1976	1,998	0	9,070	2,015	681	0	1,710	948	3,162	19,584
1977	3,164	0	9,019	2,872	2,300	0	1,998	600	12,558	32,513
1978	4,090	0	11,666	3,089	2,548	0	2,553	1,365	4,937	30,249
1979	5,238	0	14,889	4,625	653	0	2,033	964	12,523	40,925
1980	6,358	0	10,606	6,000	802	0	4,284	1,082	22,997	52,130
1981	8,542	135	15,087	15,698	1,413	0	5,046	987	15,680	62,587
1982	6,963	0	14,623	4,020	3,985	0	5,067	2,371	6,271	43,301
1983	5,354	0	11,921	−1,917	−804	0	4,586	1,980	−22,445	−1,326
1984	4,278	0	9,953	−2,035	−1,038	0	5,762	711	−9,496	8,135
1985	5,974	0	4,701	−2,082	−805	0	5,634	861	−5,302	8,980
1986	4,397	0	1,078	−1,880	−1,377	0	6,250	1,626	−3,304	6,792
1987	3,830	78	4,362	−2,292	−2,030	0	4,157	1,420	3,709	13,235
1988	7,619	176	4,196	−3,943	−1,441	0	4,176	1,663	4,194	16,640
1989	7,966	545	−3,035	−2,749	−1,229	0	4,087	1,241	2,616	9,443
1990	8,181	2,464	−447	2,315	−26	171	6,727	540	7,633	27,558
1991	12,815	6,935	460	1,354	3,099	1,216	2,979	−1,485	8,061	35,432
1992	14,800	8,109	−100	4,187	−1,842	6,580	1,197	−1,481	14,044	45,494
1993	13,850	23,352	1,734	−933	6,141	14,369	2,660	−1,572	19,333	78,933
1994	28,767	17,273	2,315	4,697	7,039	7,937	−1,498	−1,943	9,955	74,541
1995	30,500	4,770	3,158	11,314	7,820	3,491	9,143	−1,345	14,717	83,569
1996	44,311	12,186	730	15,288	25,324	7,271	−8,777	−1,601	164	94,896
1997	66,718	13,326	2,519	29,394	5,208	5,639	−4,738	−1,042	−7,663	109,363
1998	73,823	−2,170	6,380	32,732	9,001	8,291	8,360	−1,671	−27,561	107,185
1999	88,035	−3,626	−7,178	5,633	16,280	3,034	2,423	779	−7,932	97,446
2000	76,961	−453	−609	307	5,744	−537	−396	−898	−2,558	77,561
2001	69,949	2,291	−2,102	−574	2,671	966	4,796	−1,668	−13,394	62,935
2002	44,682	1,507	−5,033	−5,285	3,611	−3,112	871	−1,825	−8,988	26,427
2003	36,600	1,420	−3,564	−2,263	12,004	1,233	−1,187	−749	2,610	46,104

n.a. = not available

Source: See box 4.1.

are supplemented by grants (column 11), which consist predominantly of official aid. These built up fairly steadily until the end of the 1980s but then stagnated or declined (even in nominal terms) until quite recently. Second, capital inflows are partially offset by capital outflows, shown bro-

| | Resident outflows | | | Interest payments | | | | Interest received | Net |
Grants (11)	Bank deposits (12)	Portfolio investment (13)	Total (14)	Long-term (15)	Short-term (16)	IMF charges (17)	Earnings on FDI (18)	from abroad (19)	resource transfer (20)
133	n.a.	n.a	n.a	1,395	0	0	662	0	n.a
138	n.a	n.a	n.a	1,532	0	0	811	0	n.a
136	n.a	n.a	n.a	1,734	0	0	563	0	n.a
122	n.a	n.a	n.a	2,526	0	0	930	0	n.a
160	n.a	n.a	n.a	3,829	0	11	1,050	0	n.a
184	n.a	n.a	n.a	4,900	0	31	1,470	0	n.a
219	n.a	n.a	n.a	4,981	0	70	1,708	0	n.a
219	n.a	n.a	n.a	5,932	0	109	2,876	6	n.a
291	n.a	n.a	n.a	8,650	0	94	3,120	6	n.a
452	n.a	n.a	n.a	12,599	0	75	4,588	6	n.a
425	n.a	n.a	n.a	17,355	6,890	95	5,213	0	n.a
391	n.a	n.a	n.a	22,237	10,489	103	6,298	0	n.a
665	39,170	0	39,170	27,292	10,130	148	6,045	0	-38,820
922	13,420	0	13,420	25,733	8,545	346	4,172	0	-52,619
1,296	5,710	0	5,710	28,707	5,609	902	4,368	0	-35,865
1,527	12,410	0	12,410	28,478	5,148	1,088	4,823	0	-41,439
1,678	12,830	0	12,830	25,140	3,553	1,316	5,213	0	-39,584
2,045	12,640	0	12,640	24,829	2,377	1,083	4,620	62	-30,208
2,227	3,360	0	3,360	28,693	3,102	1,073	6,034	51	-23,344
2,254	18,320	0	18,320	20,424	3,863	1,234	8,070	343	-39,872
2,278	19,220	0	19,220	18,089	2,377	1,459	7,520	589	-18,240
4,140	-10,500	0	-10,500	17,820	4,116	1,420	7,622	891	19,987
2,599	-12,030	1,036	-10,994	17,839	3,096	1,304	8,228	746	29,366
2,827	-8,162	3,810	-4,352	17,592	4,488	1,238	10,496	974	53,273
2,575	15,088	2,293	17,381	20,909	5,530	720	14,134	1,061	19,504
3,285	1,478	8,039	9,517	28,608	6,418	1,104	15,096	1,613	27,723
3,108	1,510	7,098	8,608	30,010	7,519	1,105	15,922	1,875	36,715
2,686	6,029	10,780	16,809	33,490	6,472	928	19,979	2,971	37,340
3,171	3,037	-502	2,535	38,972	6,484	828	20,619	2,609	43,527
2,896	11,975	11,860	23,835	44,694	6,154	1,040	17,831	2,866	9,656
2,469	2,001	2,860	4,861	47,909	6,562	778	22,409	3,217	728
3,210	3,044	31,375	34,419	48,298	4,560	608	20,401	3,551	-38,590
2,730	-3,403	5,391	1,988	36,258	2,211	1,195	18,456	3,262	-27,688
2,904	4,040	19,262	23,302	34,547	1,794	1,070	16,300	2,856	-25,149

ken down between bank deposits and portfolio investment in columns 12 and 13 and summed in column 14.

Net resource transfers consist of net capital flows plus grants less the reverse flow of payments for interest and profits from past investment. Interest payments, on long-term and short-term claims respectively, are shown in columns 15 and 16. Interest paid to the IMF (IMF charges) is

Box 4.1   Capital inflows and resource transfer: Data variable descriptions

FDI

GDF 2004 Series BX.KLT.DINV.CD.DT. Foreign direct investment (net) shows the net change in foreign investment in the reporting country. Foreign direct investment is defined as investment that is made to acquire a lasting management interest (usually of at least 10 percent of voting stock) in an enterprise operating in a country other than that of the investor (defined according to residency), the investor's purpose being an effective voice in the management of the enterprise. It is the sum of equity capital, reinvestment of earnings, other long-term capital, and short-term capital as shown in the balance of payments.

Portfolio equity

GDF 2004 Series BX.PEF.TOTL.CD.DT. Portfolio equity flows are the sum of country funds, depository receipts (US or global), and direct purchases of shares by foreign investors.

Bank loans:
Public sector

GDF 2004 Series DT.NFL.PCBK.CD. Public and publicly guaranteed commercial bank loans from private banks and other private financial institutions. Net flows (or net lending or net disbursements) are disbursements minus principal repayments.

Private sector

GDF 2004 Series DT.NFL.PNGC.CD. Nonguaranteed long-term commercial bank loans from private banks and other private financial institutions. Net flows (or net lending or net disbursements) are disbursements minus principal repayments. Long-term external debt is defined as debt that has an original or extended maturity of more than one year and that is owed to nonresidents and is repayable in foreign currency, goods, or services.

Bonds:
Public sector

GDF 2004 Series DT.NFL.PBND.CD. Public and publicly guaranteed debt from bonds that are either publicly issued or privately placed. Net flows (or net lending or net disbursements) are disbursements minus principal repayments.

Private sector

GDF 2004 Series DT.NFL.PNGB.CD. Nonguaranteed long-term debt from bonds that are privately placed. Net flows (or net lending or net disbursements) are disbursements minus principal repayments. Long-term external debt is defined as debt that has an original or extended maturity of more than one year and that is owed to nonresidents and is repayable in foreign currency, goods, or services.

Other public sector debt:
Official creditors

GDF 2004 Series DT.NFL.OFFT.CD. Public and publicly guaranteed debt from official creditors includes loans from international organizations (multilateral loans) and loans from governments (bilateral loans). Loans from international organizations include loans and credits from the World Bank, regional development banks, and other multilateral and intergovernmental agencies. Excluded are loans from funds administered by

(box continues next page)

Box 4.1   *(continued)*

an international organization on behalf of a single donor government; these are classified as loans from governments. Government loans include loans from governments
and their agencies (including central banks), loans from autonomous bodies, and direct
loans from official export credit agencies. Net flows (or net lending or net disbursements) are disbursements minus principal repayments.

Private creditors
GDF 2004 Series DT.NFL.PROP.CD. Public and publicly guaranteed other private credits
from manufacturers, exporters, and other suppliers of goods, and bank credits covered
by a guarantee of an export credit agency. Net flows (or net lending or net disbursements) are disbursements minus principal repayments.

Short-term debt
GDF 2004 Series DT.NFL.DSTC.CD. Net flows (or net lending or net disbursements) of
short-term debt are disbursements minus principal repayments. Short-term external
debt is defined as debt that has an original maturity of one year or less. Available data
permit no distinction between public and private nonguaranteed short-term debt.

Total net inflows
Sum columns listed above.

Grants
GDF 2004 Series BX.GRT.EXTA.CD.DT. Grants are defined as legally binding commitments that obligate a specific value of funds available for disbursement for which there
is no repayment requirement.

Resident outflows:
Bank deposits
1981–94 IMF IFS Table 7xrd (Cross-Border Bank Deposits of Nonbanks by Residence
of Depositor) from IFS *Yearbook 1995* (Note this is the last year in which these data were
published by the IMF). 1995–2003, table 7B (External Loans and Deposits of Reporting
Banks Vis-a-Vis Individual Countries, Liabilities, Estimated Exchange Rate Adjusted
Changes) from the Bank for International Settlements (BIS) *International Banking Statistics* (4 quarters of changes). Note that due to change in data gathering entity, there
is a break in the series from 1994–95 and the 1995 number is the change in liabilities
from Q4 1995 to Q1 1996 from the BIS table 7B. Due to lack of conformity in country
coverage among sources (IMF IFS, BIS *International Banking Statistics* and the World
Bank *Global Development Finance*), other sources (IMF and BIS) have been aligned as
closely as coverage allows to the precise country coverage of the GDF database.

Portfolio investment
IMF Balance of Payments data, October 2004, Portfolio Investment Assets, End-of-
Period-Stocks (EPS), annual change. Warning: Data included for relevant countries
where available. Included are 57 countries, included in the GDF database and for which
data are reported in the IMF Balance of Payments Data. First year of data for each series excluded, if data reporting begins only during the time period covered by the time
series. Due to changes in data collection for Argentine data after 2000, changes in
Argentina's other sectors' other investment assets has been included. See IMF 2001
BOPS, part 3, "Descriptive Notes for Argentina" for further information.

(box continues next page)

Box 4.1 Capital inflows and resource transfer: Data variable descriptions *(continued)*

Total
Sum of resident outflows: Bank deposits and portfolio investment.

Interest payments:
Long-term
GDF 2004 Series DT.INT.DLXF.CD. Interest payments on long-term debt are actual amounts of interest paid in foreign currency, goods, or services in the year specified. Long-term external debt is defined as debt that has an original or extended maturity of more than one year and that is owed to nonresidents and is repayable in foreign currency, goods, or services.

Short-term
GDF 2004 Series DT.INT.DSTC.CD. Interest payments on short-term debt are actual amounts of interest paid in foreign currency, goods, or services in the year specified on short-term debt. Short-term external debt is defined as debt that has an original maturity of one year or less. Available data permit no distinction between public and private nonguaranteed short-term debt.

IMF charges
GDF 2004 Series DT.INT.DIMF.CD. IMF charges cover interest payments with respect to all uses of IMF resources, excluding those resulting from drawings in the reserve tranche.

Earnings on FDI
GDF 2004 Series BX.KLT.DREM.CD.DT. Profit remittances on direct foreign investment are the sum of reinvested earnings on direct investment and other direct investment income and are part of net transfers.

Interest received from abroad
Data from IMF Balance of Payments October 2004 Database Series PORTFOLIO INVESTMENT INCOME: CRE and PI INCOME ON EQUITY (DIVIDENDS): CRE. Included are developing countries also included in the GDF Database. Warning: Data included for relevant countries where available.

Net resource transfer
Total net inflows, plus grants, minus total resident outflows, all interest payments, IMF charges and earnings on FDI, and plus interest received from abroad.

Sources: World Bank, *Global Development Finance*, 2004; IMF, *International Financial Statistics*; IMF, *Balance of Payments Statistics.*

---

separately shown in column 17. Profits made by multinationals are shown in column 18; this figure in principle includes retained earnings plowed back into new investment, with the retained earnings appearing as a new capital inflow in column 1. Finally, interest earned by developing country residents on their foreign assets is shown in column 19. The net resource transfer (column 20) is the sum of columns 10, 11, and 19, minus the sum of columns 14, 15, 16, 17, and 18. It is the sum that developing countries could spend in augmenting absorption, or building up reserves, as a result of the grants they receive and their old and new capital account transactions with the rest of the world.

Volatility

Which of these flows contribute to the boom-bust cycle, and which of them are relatively stable or even contracyclical? My colleagues Wendy Dobson and Gary Hufbauer (2001) surveyed the literature, provided citations to it, and laid out the resulting conventional wisdom. They concluded that official capital varies in a stabilizing way, that FDI provides a pretty stable source of finance, that portfolio investment tends to accentuate crises, and that the biggest source of instability comes from the variations in bank lending. Do those conclusions seem to be consistent with the data shown in tables 4.1 through 4.3?

Certainly it seems that official loans (column 7) played a stabilizing role again during the recent crises. Likewise FDI remained relatively stable, although it fell off in Latin America between 1999 and 2003. This fall was aggravated, however, by the passing of the peak in privatization, and it is difficult to know how much is a reflection of the region's cyclical difficulties. The figures show portfolio equity falling sharply during the crisis, and again in 2001, but remaining positive in aggregate although the regional totals have moved into negative territory at times. Bank lending turned sharply negative, as did bonds issued by the private sector and short-term debt. Resident outflows, also known as capital flight, also increased substantially in 1997, although they rather surprisingly turned around in 1998 and fluctuated sharply from year to year thereafter. All this seems consistent with Dobson and Hufbauer's conventional wisdom, especially since much of the bank lending is short term and therefore appears in column 9 in the tables.

Another question one might ask is what sort of capital inflow would be neither too little nor too much but about right. The average net inflow (column 10) for the past 10 years has been about $210 billion, of which some $150 billion has been in the form of FDI, $16 billion in portfolio equity, $14 billion in bank loans to the private sector, and $20 billion in bonds to the public sector, plus sums averaging less than $10 billion a year under the other headings. Had flows been reasonably stable close to those levels, it would have been difficult to argue that big problems would have arisen from the inflows; even the increase in bank lending to the private sector could have been largely accounted for by the secular increase in trade credit. It is the extreme variability around those levels that made the capital account a problem.

Comparison of Six Characteristics

The beginning of the chapter identified six dimensions in which various forms of capital flow differ. This section offers a systematic comparison of the different forms of capital flow in each of these dimensions.

Cost

Official capital (plus the limited sums provided by foreign NGOs) tends to be cheapest, especially (obviously) when in the form of grants or highly concessional loans. But even the commercial terms on which the MDBs lend in their regular operations often include an element of subsidy, as the IFIAC report (2000) went to great length to demonstrate. The guarantee provided by the developed members of the MDBs in the form of their callable capital enables the MDBs to borrow and on-lend on AAA terms that most developing countries could not hope to replicate. Supplier credits may also involve some concessional element, although the Berne Union has in recent years curbed the competition among its members to win export orders by offering cheap credit.

At the other extreme is believed to be FDI. Official estimates of the return on FDI do not exist, but a conservative estimate of the return on US FDI in 1998 was approximately 12.4 percent. This takes the return as consisting of US reported direct investment receipts of $102.8 billion, adds half of the reported license and royalty fees of $36.8 billion, and deflates by the book value of US FDI of $980.6 billion. The market value is undoubtedly larger than this, but if one were to use market value as base, then one should add the year's increase in market value to the return. The above figures probably underestimate the rate of return because transfer pricing is used to reduce reported profits.

Rates of return on portfolio equity (which include capital gains as well as dividends) tend to be extremely variable, reflecting the volatility of stock markets in general and of emerging markets in particular. The fact that markets demand an equity risk premium implies that one would expect that, on average, the return on portfolio equity would be higher than that on loan capital, essentially because the "lenders" are taking more of the risks. One reflection of this is that dividends tend to be low when a country is confronting macroeconomic problems, thus redistributing the foreign exchange cost of servicing foreign capital toward times when one would expect the country to be in a better position to pay. Because a large part of the return also consists of increases in the value of shares, the cost of debt service also tends to be delayed, presumably to a time when the country's marginal rate of time preference will be lower.

It is not clear that any systematic difference exists between the cost of bank loans versus bonds. However, borrowing on longer maturities tends to be more expensive than short-term borrowing.

Conditionality

The only explicit conditionality is that required by the official sector, especially by the IMF. The conditionality required by the World Bank and the regional development banks is also, at times, of the macroeconomic character typical of IMF programs, or it may be related to sectoral policies, or it is still in some cases confined to the design and implementation of a particular project. Whatever the project or program, it is always accompanied by the need to negotiate terms with the MDB in question. The desire to escape from the tutelage of the MDBs is usually reckoned to have been one of the factors that drove the explosion of bank lending in the 1970s. Those of us who have worked for the MDBs and believe that their conditionality is by and large well conceived tend to regard this desire as having been a costly, if understandable, mistake. Bilateral grants or loans may also have a series of conditions attached to their disbursement.

The work of David Dollar and his colleagues (World Bank 1998) has emphasized the key importance of local ownership of a program of policy reform, which led the MDBs to question the value of conditionality that is imposed rather than provide a means of allowing a country to precommit. World Bank authors have therefore argued (see, for example, Collier 2000) that the safest way of ensuring that lending goes only to countries that are genuinely committed to good policies is to lend on the basis of performance rather than promises.

The other form of lending that sometimes comes with something akin to conditionality is FDI, which may involve a negotiation between the host-country government (or local authority, or both) and the multinational enterprise contemplating an investment. But in this case the conditionality may be two-way: While the multinational may (for example) make its investment conditional on stipulated improvements in infrastructure, the host country may also (for example) impose performance requirements. At least that might have been true in the past, although the Uruguay Round agreements circumscribed the ability of World Trade Organization members to impose performance requirements.

Other forms of capital inflow are free of any conditionality, except perhaps for the requirement that the borrower implement the project supposedly being financed (the word "supposedly" reflects the fact of fungibility).

Risk Bearing

The parties to an investment financed by foreign capital presumably have some more or less well-defined expectations regarding the revenues that will result from the investment and the costs that will be involved in servicing the foreign capital at the time when the investment is contracted. But because we live in an uncertain world, the actual revenue and cost streams will typically differ from those expected at the time the contract is agreed. The question is: Who will reap the benefits if the revenues are larger or the costs smaller; conversely, who will suffer if revenues are smaller or costs larger than was expected at the time of the contract?

One may break down these risks into three components:

- **Commercial risk** refers to the risk of the revenue stream being different from that anticipated as a result of higher or lower prices or sales, or higher or lower nonfinancial costs.

- **Interest risk** refers to the risk of interest rates being different from those anticipated, which would result in a fixed interest rate being more or less advantageous to the lender than anticipated, or a variable interest rate imposing larger or smaller costs on the borrower.

- **Exchange rate risk** refers to the possibility of the exchange rate between the borrower's currency and the lender's currency varying from that anticipated, which would mean (ceteris paribus) that a given stream of debt service payments would be worth more or less to the lender, or would cost more or less than expected to the borrower.

The question is: Who bears these three risks under various forms of capital flow?

Almost all official flows, with the exception of investments by the International Finance Corporation or analogous regional institutions, concentrate commercial risks on the borrower. The same is true of supplier credits and of bank loans and bonds to sovereigns. Loans and bonds to private-sector borrowers allow commercial risk to be passed on to the lender only in the most extreme circumstances—when the borrower declares bankruptcy. Equity flows, both direct and portfolio, are very different in this respect: Commercial risk is assumed by the investor. The flow of profits and, thus, the income of the investor depend on the trading outcome of the borrower. In addition, changes in expectations of future commercial outcomes influence the value of the assets held by the investor; this is particularly obvious in the case of portfolio equity, but the same would be true of FDI if it were marked-to-market.

Equity investors also bear interest risk. The location of interest risk on loans depends upon whether the loan carries a fixed or floating (i.e., periodically adjustable) interest rate. A fixed interest rate places this risk on the lender, who receives an above-market stream of interest if the market interest rate falls below that expected at the time of the contract but who suffers correspondingly in the event of an interest rate rise. A variable interest rate relocates that risk to the borrower, who benefits in the event of lower-than-expected interest rates and suffers in the event that interest rates rise.[6] Most official loans carry a fixed interest rate, which places interest risk on the lender. Most bank loans, and some bonds as well, carry a floating interest rate, which passes the risk to the borrower.

Equity investors also carry exchange rate risk, although their real transactions may provide an effective hedge against this risk. In most other cases, the exchange rate risk is carried by the borrower, except when developing countries borrow in their own currency. This has proved in recent years to be a potent source of risk (Goldstein and Turner 2004). In particular, when the borrower's currency is devalued, the borrower suddenly finds that its liabilities as measured in domestic currency have increased. Unless the borrower has a natural hedge, for example, in the form of a stream of foreign currency receipts from exporting, its net worth and therefore creditworthiness diminishes. Such currency mismatches were one of the major reasons that the East Asian crisis proved so devastating in 1997.

The bottom line reflects a point that has been emphasized by Kenneth Rogoff (1999): Equity investments are a good way of shifting risk from the borrower to the lender.

Intellectual Property

The distinguishing feature of FDI is that the multinational corporation brings with it access to one form or another of intellectual property: technology embodied in patents or know-how, trademarks, foreign markets, or managerial expertise. Without some form of intellectual property to exploit, it is difficult to understand how a foreign corporation could expect to get the upper hand over local rivals with their natural advantage of greater familiarity with local circumstances.

The only other forms of capital flow that might bring some of the advantages of access to intellectual property are official capital and capital originating with NGOs. Both the MDBs and some NGOs like to regard themselves as having special expertise in access to knowledge as well as the ability to transfer it.

---

6. Strictly speaking, one should be referring here to real rather than nominal interest rates. Thus, a higher nominal interest rate that reflects higher inflation that inflates the borrower's receipts and nonfinancial costs equally will leave the borrower's and lender's net worth unchanged (although it will still have a real effect in reducing the effective maturity of the loan). This suggests that variable interest rates are an effective way of reducing the risk of both borrower and lender when the main source of interest risk stems from variations in inflation. An even more effective strategy is to index the loan to inflation, which avoids shortening the maturity of the debt when inflation increases and also distinguishes between interest changes that reflect changes in inflation and those that stem from real factors.

Impact on Investment

Econometric evidence indicates that FDI is translated 100 percent, or perhaps rather more (presumably because it crowds in complementary local investment), into an increase in investment (UNCTAD, *World Investment Report 1999*, 172). An inflow of portfolio equity investment bids up the price of shares and thus reduces the cost of capital (Bekaert, Harvey, and Lumsdaine 1999); there is now also strong econometric evidence that this feeds through into increased physical investment, as noted in chapter 3.

In contrast, all other forms of capital inflow go partly into reserve accumulation and partly into an increased current account deficit, with the increase in absorption that the latter represents typically being split between investment and consumption in much the same proportion as an increase in income. Therefore, if a country wants to use foreign capital to stimulate investment and growth rather than to redistribute consumption over time, its preference should be for FDI, followed by portfolio equity.

Vulnerability to Capital Flow Reversal

The financial crises that developing countries have experienced since the outbreak of the debt crisis in 1982 have compelled the conclusion that one of the major disadvantages of capital mobility is that it makes countries vulnerable to a peremptory reversal in the flow of capital. Conventional wisdom has long held that some forms of capital flow are much more liable to rapid reversal than others. This view was challenged in a paper by Claessens, Dooley, and Warner (1994), who failed to find statistically significant differences in the time-series properties of different forms of capital flow (FDI, portfolio equity, long-term, short-term, banks, government, and private). But in his discussion of this paper, Guillermo Calvo presciently pointed out that the authors' estimates of volatility (which essentially focused on the second moment of the time series) might fail to give due weight to what is of most importance, the possibility of occasional major disruptions (which are measured by higher moments in the time series). In East Asia during its recent crisis (see table 4.2), FDI was largely maintained while bank capital reversed on a grand scale; this leads to the judgment that it is indeed proper to worry much more about the volatility of some forms of capital flow than of others.

FDI has traditionally been regarded as the most stable form of capital inflow, and recent experience substantiates this view. One should expect that multinationals will hedge their local currency exposure when they sense a weakness in the domestic economy, and they will surely seek to shift working balances among currencies depending on their view of macroeconomic prospects. The question is whether such shifts will be large relative to the total sum sunk in capital investment. One should also ask whether these shifts are large because of the size of FDI. A multinational could in principle speculate against an emerging-market currency even if it had not made any investment in that country; it is only insofar as bigger past FDI induces it to undertake more hedging or to increase its willingness to build up a short position that it is correct to regard the stability of recorded FDI as misleading.

Official capital flows have also traditionally been viewed as relatively stable, and indeed the evidence is that they are contracyclical.

Bank lending, which constituted the principal component of the capital flow reversal in East Asia, is at the other extreme from official finance. The same was true during the debt crisis of the 1980s. Common sense (and received wisdom) suggest that short-term bank loans are likely to be more unstable than long-term loans, an expectation that would again seem to have been reinforced by the evaporation of interbank credit lines experienced by Korea in 1997. One reason that Claessens, Dooley, and Warner (1994) failed to find any distinction in volatility based on maturity may be that trade credits are included in the statistics with other short-term credits extended by banks. In fact, trade credits are usually considered to be one of the least volatile sources of finance, despite the fact that each individual credit is short-term, because under normal circumstances (though not in some of the East Asian countries in 1997) they are constantly renewed as new trade transactions come to be financed.

It is the residual item—nontrade-related bank claims, which have a short term to maturity—that conventional wisdom holds to be particularly volatile. It has been argued by Avinash Persaud (2000) that the recent moves to strengthen bank risk management and prudential standards and to increase transparency may even intensify the problem of procyclical behavior by banks. He points to the increasing use of daily earnings at risk (DEAR) limits as a tool of risk management that seems perfectly rational when viewed from the standpoint of the individual bank but that can work to increase volatility. The DEAR sets a limit on how much a bank is prepared to risk losing over the following day with, say, 1 percent probability:

> It is calculated by taking the bank's portfolio . . . and estimating the future distribution of daily returns based on past measures of market correlation and volatility. Both rising volatility and rising correlation will increase the potential loss of the portfolio, increasing DEAR. . . . When DEAR exceeds the limit, the bank reduces exposure, often by switching into less volatile and less correlated assets.

Daily publication of statistics can accelerate and intensify the spread of any bad news that may break, with declining asset values and increasing volatility serving as sophisticated positive feedback mechanisms.

Concern is often expressed about the potential volatility of other claims that can be sold quickly, including portfolio equity and long-term bonds as well as short-term instruments. Table 4.2 does indeed show a reversal in the flow of portfolio investment to East Asia in 1997–98, although with nothing like the size or duration of the reversal seen in the case of bank lending. One should expect less volatility in the case of portfolio equity than in the case of short-term loans for one important reason: The price of the relevant asset (shares) can adjust; all the adjustment need not take place in the volume. Indeed, if a shock has an identical impact on the future expectations of domestic and foreign investors in shares, one would expect that all the resulting adjustment would show up in a change in share prices, with no consequences for capital flows or exchange rates. (I would also argue that the stock market is a good place to absorb the impact of changes in expectations because the links from the stock market to the real economy tend to be weak in the short term.) It is only when foreign investors lose their nerve about the prospects for a country or a region in a way that domestic investors do not that one should expect an impact on capital flows. Perhaps that happened in East Asia in 1997, since a number of empirical studies of portfolio equity investment are less reassuring than these considerations would have led one to expect.

Specifically, Kenneth Froot, Paul O'Connell, and Mark Seasholes (1998) found evidence that equity flows are persistent over time and that investors often buy (sell) in response to a price rise (decline). Kaminsky, Lyons, and Schmukler (2000) concluded that mutual funds have had a destabilizing impact and have helped spread contagion in Latin America. It also seems that Chilean pension funds made almost no use of their new rights to invest abroad during Chile's capital inflow surge but later began placing funds abroad on a big scale when capital flow reversal occurred after the East Asian crisis (Ffrench-Davis and Tapia 2001). Bekaert, Harvey, and Lumsdaine (1999) find that, when equity capital leaves, it does so faster than when it entered, suggesting that it is not after all so difficult to find domestic purchasers.

Only Michael Barth and Xin Zhang (1999) found no evidence that foreign investors had played a destabilizing role; indeed, they claim (201) that in only one month, December 1997, were mutual funds net sellers in the four main crisis countries of East Asia. Although they refer (199) to some investors being attracted "into the Asian markets with a short-term horizon seeking high returns," they also argue (202–5) that the figures show that foreign institutional investors were slow to exit after the crisis started, as a result of which they lost a lot of money.

Korea has a particularly rich dataset that has enabled investigators to trace the strategy of individual investors in a way that is not possible elsewhere. The first study to exploit this source, Choe, Kho, and Stulz (1998), was somewhat reassuring in that it suggested that, although the trades of foreign investors were destabilizing before the crisis, the foreign investors acted as a stabilizing force during the crisis. However, their data extended only briefly into the crisis period, and the subsequent study by Woochan

Kim and Shang-Jin Wei (1999a) concluded that foreign institutional and (even more) individual investors had been positive feedback traders (i.e., had bought in response to a price rise and sold in response to a price fall) both before and during the crisis. The only exception occurred before the crisis by those foreign institutions that had Korean offices; these were contrarian traders (i.e., they had tended to buy recent losers and sell recent winners). In that study, Kim and Wei also calculated that a contrarian strategy would have been more profitable than a positive-feedback strategy, which suggests that the Koreans who must perforce have been following a contrarian strategy (as the counterpart of the foreign positive-feedback strategies) must have made money, or at least lost less money, compared with the foreigners. Kim and Wei (1999b) also found evidence that mutual funds based in the United States and the United Kingdom engaged in positive-feedback trading and, to some extent, in herding behavior in Korea in 1997–98.

Note that all these studies focus on portfolio equity investment in the stock markets of emerging countries. As Barth and Zhang (1999) point out, portfolio equity is invested in emerging markets through two other channels as well. One is in the form of private (i.e., nontraded) equity. Barth and Zhang's figure 6-2 suggests that in East Asia this is a small but rather stable flow. The other channel is by emerging-market companies listing their shares on international markets like New York (of dominant importance for Latin American companies) or London (ditto for South African companies). Barth and Zhang's table 6-12 shows that international placements became of major importance in the mid-1990s and peaked in 1997, although they fell substantially in 1998. The decline in international placements was nevertheless modest compared with local investment: International placements went from $6 billion in 1996 to $11 billion in 1997 to $4 billion in 1998, while local investment fell from $9 billion in 1996 to minus $3 billion in 1997 to plus $1 billion in 1998.

As shown in table 4.2, there was a sharp reduction in the inflow of portfolio equity into East Asia during the 1997 crisis. Reportedly (and consistent with the report of Barth and Zhang 1999, 197) this reflects quite different behavior on the part of two different groups of investors. The withdrawals were made by crossover funds[7] that had been searching for high-yielding investments and had been attracted by the high yields in East Asian share markets before the crisis but that had not advertised their investments in emerging markets. They were embarrassed to be holding assets whose value collapsed, and they got out as fast as they could, before their holdings became widely known and criticized. But the holdings by funds that specialized in investments in emerging markets re-

---

7. Crossover funds are those that have not declared their intent of restricting their investments to a particular asset class or geographical region and are free to switch where they place money without breaching trust with their investors.

mained steady and may even have picked up some of the shares being sold by the former group, perhaps to sustain their target asset allocations. These investors, aware that these are inherently risky markets that will have downs as well as ups, are in emerging markets for the long haul, and neither the managers of the funds nor their investors panicked.

Does Milton Friedman's famous 1953 theorem, which says that destabilizing speculators must lose money (because to destabilize a market one must buy near the peak and sell near the trough, whereas making money requires the opposite), reassure one that funds that amplify the boom-bust cycle will lose money and thereby at least enrich domestic investors? Not necessarily. The counterpart to sales by foreigners might possibly be purchases by other foreigners. But even if foreign portfolio investors do indeed on balance follow the herd—buying when the market is rising and selling when it is falling—so that overall domestic investors are selling when the market is rising and buying when it is falling, it does not necessarily follow that the foreigners will lose money. Buying on a rising market and buying near the peak are not the same thing; speculators who are alert to changes in trends may be able to quit buying, sell out soon after the peak is past, and thereby make money. The empirical studies reported above offer contradictory verdicts on whether many foreign investors in fact got out of East Asia sufficiently quickly to save their skins.

What is quite clear is that foreign investors in total lost an enormous sum of money in East Asia: some $166 billion during 1997, according to the calculations of Barth and Zhang (1999, 204). There seems to be enough evidence that foreign investment in portfolio equity could have been destabilizing to conclude that these losses were at least in part self-inflicted. To the extent that is true, investors as well as the capital-importing countries would collectively stand to benefit from policies that succeed in curbing capital flow reversals.

Much the same analysis applies to long-term bonds as well as to portfolio equity because bond prices can also fluctuate in response to changes in expectations in such a way as to ensure that the total stock of bonds continues to be held. However, there does not appear to be a similar literature examining what happened to foreign holdings of bonds during the Asian crisis. One fact to note is that what are nominally long-term bonds sometimes include put options, giving the holder the right to demand early repayment at the holder's discretion on certain dates. If such dates coincide with a crisis, the loan tends to disappear just when money is most needed, as happened in Korea in late 1997.

Summary

Table 4.4 offers a summary of the judgments expressed above. It shows that official capital tends to be cheap but subject to conditionality, which

Table 4.4 Characteristics of different forms of capital flows

Form of capital flows	Costs	Conditionality	Risk bearing			Access to intellectual property	Impact on investment	Vulnerability to capital flow reversals
			Commercial risk	Interest rate risk	Exchange rate risk			
FDI	High	Two-way	Lender	Lender	Lender	Yes	Yes	Minimal
Portfolio equity	Fairly high	No	Lender	Lender	Lender	No	Yes	Apparently
Bonds and banks	Medium	No	Borrower	Fixed: lender Floating: borrower	Foreign exchange denominated: borrower Local currency denominated: lender	No	No	Yes, especially short term
Official lenders	Low	Yes	Borrower	Lender	Borrower	Possibly	No	No, anticyclical

is another way of saying that it may bring some limited intellectual capital with it. While it does not involve risk sharing (except for interest risk), it is not subject to capital flow reversals; indeed, MDB lending at least tends to be stabilizing. A counterpart to these attractions, from the standpoint of the borrower, is that official capital is rationed by the limited supply available. FDI is expensive but the borrower gets some very real advantages in return: full risk sharing, access to intellectual property, a big impact on investment, and minimal exposure to the danger of capital flow reversal. Portfolio equity also tends to be expensive, but it too has good risk-sharing properties, adds to investment, and perhaps somewhat limits exposure to capital flow reversal. Loans, from banks or via bonds, are cheaper than equity finance and have no conditionality, but they have little impact on investment and bring no access to intellectual property. They are highly vulnerable to capital flow reversal. They necessarily place commercial risk on the borrower, but where interest risk and exchange risk lie depends on the nature of the contract. The most common form of bank lending, with a floating interest rate and denomination in foreign exchange, places both risks on the borrower. Conversely, a fixed interest rate and denomination in local currency would shift those risks to the lender. It is worth pausing to ask why this arrangement is so uncommon.

Why Do Emerging Markets Borrow Short-Term in Dollars?

It is a fact that most developing countries, including most of the more advanced ones usually referred to as emerging markets, do much of their foreign borrowing in a form—dollar-denominated and short-term—that has the effect of imposing both exchange risk and interest risk on the borrower. The risks involved are substantial, given that the borrowing is essentially undertaken to finance a long-term project (called development). The risks are particularly serious in the form of currency mismatching. Why do countries expose themselves to these risks?

Consider first why countries choose to borrow in dollars (or some other international currency) rather than local currency. The most usual explanation is that it is cheaper. Most sovereigns, and even more so most corporations, are most easily able to borrow in their local currency by selling local-currency bonds in their local market. The supply of funds may be greater relative to the demand for funds, leading to lower interest rates, in major international financial centers than in local markets. Moreover, most of the funds in local markets usually come from local sources, so that borrowing in local markets may not bring much of an inflow of foreign exchange, which the government may be seeking when it issues sovereign debt.

Many economists have emphasized that a sovereign that borrows in its own currency is subject to moral hazard because it is able to reduce the real cost of servicing its debt by inflating it away. There are ample historical cases where emerging-market borrowers (including some that have now emerged) behaved that way (see, for example, Reinhart, Rogoff, and Savastano 2003). Hence, until the borrower or its government is fully trusted by the international market, it may be able to borrow from foreign sources in its own currency only if the debt is indexed (which curtails a borrower's ability to default on debt through inflation). Another possible factor is that the local markets of emerging-market countries often have an incomplete financial infrastructure, which would expose a foreign lender in those markets to risks that the lender is not used to incurring and does not know how to deal with. It is not simply that investors do not fully trust an emerging-market government to fulfill its legal contract and not deliberately subvert it through inflation; in addition, there may not be a legally satisfactory way of writing a contract in the local market.

One influential school of thought (Eichengreen and Hausmann 2003) has taken this to the extreme of claiming that countries borrow the way they do because they have no options. These countries suffer from "original sin," a term intended to signify that no other type of foreign lending is available to them (see chapter 6). The fact is, however, that emerging markets are increasingly borrowing in their local markets in bonds denominated in their own currencies, and foreigners are getting accustomed to the idea of buying such bonds.[8] It is easy to understand the difficulties (described in the preceding paragraph) that impede rapid progress along this road, but it is quite unpersuasive to assert that the obstacles are permanent and irremovable. Borrowers that have tried issuing domestic currency debt in international markets (as the Banco do Brasil did in December 2004 and the Colombian government did in early 2005) have discovered that this is not impossible.

It has also been claimed that companies may actually find that it is less risky to issue debt denominated in dollars than debt in their local currency (Jeanne 2003). The crucial hypothesis is that arbitrage will keep the domestic interest rate adjusted for the risk of devaluation equal to (or above) the international interest rate, so that the domestic interest rate will rise as devaluation risk increases. This means that a company that finances itself by domestic borrowing faces a risk of bankruptcy that may increase as the risk of devaluation increases; if devaluation does not occur, the extra cost of having borrowed domestically could be sufficient to push the company into insolvency. It is impossible to deny that this could occur, because Jeanne has built a model in which it does, but it does look somewhat improbable: The increase in devaluation risk will also mean

---

8. It is believed that foreigners now own something like 40 percent of Mexico's 10-year bonds and as much as 70 percent of its 20-year bonds, both of which are denominated in Mexican pesos.

that the likelihood of a company being stuck with expensive domestic currency debt will fall.[9]

Consider next the issue of interest risk. The standard notion for many years has been that countries borrow short term rather than long term because it is cheaper. It is asserted that international capital markets charge a high risk premium on long-term debt, perhaps because lenders know that governments change and there is some probability that a new government will behave in a populist way no matter how responsible the current team may be. Lenders charge this to private borrowers as well as to sovereigns because the ability of corporations to service their debts depends on government policies as well as corporate solvency. Recently this theory has been formalized by Broner, Lorenzoni, and Schmukler (2004). They define the difference between the risk premiums of long-term and short-term bonds as the "term premium" and show that the term premium should, according to their model, be higher during financial crises (a prediction consistent with the facts).

Another theory that seeks to explain why countries expose themselves to the risk inherent in short-term borrowing in order to finance long-term projects sees short-term debt as a commitment device. Olivier Jeanne (2000) presents a model in which a government may issue short-term debt precisely because such debt disciplines the government and forces it to eschew the temptation to take actions that would prejudice its ability to maintain debt service. According to this view, investors could rationally refuse to buy long-term debt even though this would avoid the risk of a self-fulfilling crisis because it would also enable the government to splurge and, in this way, undermine its long-run solvency.[10]

Does it make sense to finance a long-term investment project by short-term borrowing with the expectation of being able to roll it over almost indefinitely? When a government is convinced that the market is taking an unreasonably pessimistic view of the country's prospects, it is understandable why that government would not wish to expose its citizens to the costs of high interest rates for a period of many years. Better to borrow short term for a limited time and then refinance with long-term debt when normality is restored. Doubtless there will be occasions when a government entertains unrealistic hopes of a crisis-free recovery, and this strategy will turn out to be more expensive *ex post* than immediate resort to long-term finance would have been, but it is difficult to say that no country should ever adopt this strategy. When starting from a situation of normality, however, the strategy of borrowing short term to finance a

---

9. However, Jeanne's basic thesis—that the difficulty and cost of domestic currency borrowing is largely a result of past monetary mismanagement—is persuasive enough.

10. A similar model is developed in section 3.4 of Rodrik and Velasco (1999).

long-term project amounts to a gamble that rollover will always be possible. Failure to roll over in any period will negate the benefit of having obtained external rather than internal finance for the project. On this logic, there is a clear preference for long-term finance unless (as in a trade transaction) the project really is self-liquidating within a short time period.

Policy Implications

In the light of the above analysis, should an attempt to limit the boom-bust cycle focus primarily on altering the mix of different forms of capital flow or on altering the characteristics of particular forms of flow?

One thing that stands out regarding the different forms of flow is the almost complete absence of compensating virtues attached to short-term loans, from banks or in the form of bonds, that might compensate for the exposure to capital flow reversals that they bring. As just noted, short-term loans have no conditionality (a dubious virtue) but also no risk-sharing properties and little impact on investment, and they bring no access to intellectual property. Their one clear advantage is that their interest rate tends to be relatively low; a second, but much more debatable, advantage is that they expose the borrower to continuous discipline by the financial markets. However, if one is serious about trying to curb the boom-bust cycle and believes that the relevant government is willing to discipline itself, the drawbacks of short-term loans are so large as to justify discouraging this form of capital flow.

A second lesson is the danger of loans denominated in foreign currency. It has been argued that these are not necessarily more dangerous than domestic currency loans, but the argument seems contrived. The most obvious motivation for resorting to such loans is that they are usually cheaper, and they are cheaper precisely because they shift risk to the borrower. If one wants to reduce the risk to which emerging markets are exposed, then one should try to reduce currency mismatching.

Another lesson is the advantage of inflows taking the form of equity claims rather than loans. Admittedly FDI is expensive and portfolio equity can be volatile despite the fact that stock prices adjust in a way that penalizes cutting and running, but the benefits of equity capital still outweigh the costs. However, the major thrust of the recommendations made in chapters 6 and 7 is to seek to limit the volatility of particular forms of flow rather than to rely principally on changing the mix of the flow.

5

The Asset Management Industry

Portfolio investment consists of that which takes place by the purchase of marketable securities, both bonds and equity. Portfolio investment in emerging markets has increased dramatically in the past 15 years. Reasons for this are summarized in the following long sentence (Eichengreen and Mussa 1998, 5).

> These developments reflect technological change, which has reduced the cost of issuing and trading securitized financial instruments; privatization, which has created a population of profit-oriented companies in which it is attractive to invest; far-reaching deregulation of financial markets in key industrial countries in the 1980s and early 1990s, which played an important role in allowing developing countries to raise capital in the forms of bonds and equity; the growth of institutional investors like pension funds and mutual funds with an appetite for foreign securities; and macroeconomic and trade reform in developing countries, which has rendered emerging markets more attractive to investors seeking to diversify internationally.

This chapter contains a description of the ways in which the capital markets are organized. It identifies the problems that arise as a result of the organization of the asset management industry so as to provide a background for the subsequent discussion of reforms that might stabilize the flow of capital to emerging markets.

How Asset Management Is Organized

Perhaps the most important purpose of the financial system is to intermediate funds from savers or, more accurately, from wealth owners to borrowers. One thinks of wealth owners as primarily households, but many types of organizations also have assets to invest for the long term (e.g., foundations and endowments) or to hold until needed (e.g., corporations and governmental units). Borrowers constitute corporations, public-sector entities, nonprofit organizations, and households. They may borrow by taking nonmarketable loans,[1] by issuing bonds[2] or short-term fixed interest debt, or, in the case of corporations, by issuing equities, which are ownership claims. These entitle their holders to share in the residual profits after all expenses, including those of servicing the corporation's debt, have been paid. Both bonds and equities are normally marketable, meaning they are traded on active markets at prices that fluctuate to equate supply and demand, that is, at prices that ensure that the outstanding stock of securities is willingly held. Both bonds and equities may also be issued privately (unregistered), but these are rarely traded.

Some securities are bought and held directly by wealth owners, but (at least in the United States and some of the other major industrial countries) the majority are held by financial intermediaries, or asset managers, who finance their purchases by issuing claims to the public. The most familiar of these intermediaries are banks, which issue claims fixed in nominal value and keep the bulk of their assets in direct nonmarketable loans but which also hold some marketable claims, either bonds or short-term assets like certificates of deposit (or, in some countries, also equities). Some of the other financial intermediaries, notably the savings and loans, are quite banklike in that they too issue liabilities fixed in nominal value and hold a large volume of nonmarketable claims with fixed nominal values. Indeed, they are sometimes classified together with banks as depositary institutions.

The main asset managers are (life) insurance companies, pension funds, mutual funds, hedge funds, and portfolio managers. All of these except defined-benefit pension plans and fixed-value insurance policies differ from banks in that the liabilities they issue in order to acquire the funds they manage are not fixed in nominal value. Most of the assets they acquire are marketable securities with prices that fluctuate on some market from day to day, although several of these asset managers may also place a part of their portfolios in private equity. Thus, an open-end mutual fund can be sold at the redemption value of the securities held by the fund on behalf of the purchaser. A defined-contribution pension fund promises to pay a pension equal to the annuity that can be bought by the sum (including accrued interest and capital gains) the contributor has accumu-

---

1. This is essentially the only option for households and nonprofit organizations although that statement needs to be qualified by noting that mortgages or credit card debt may be packaged by investment banks so as to form the backing for marketable securities.

2. Bonds are usually defined as relatively long-term, fixed-interest assets. Fixed interest nowadays does not mean exactly what it says because bonds may pay an interest rate that is periodically revised in accordance with some specified formula (such as the London Interbank Offered Rate, LIBOR, or the increase in some price index plus x percent).

lated. The investors in a hedge fund are entitled to withdraw their share of the fund's value on a defined date.

Asset managers may also manage funds that they receive from other financial intermediaries rather than directly from the public. These portfolio managers run what are usually referred to as boutiques. They form a key part of the system of financial intermediation but, presumably because they do not deal directly with the public, they receive little public notice. They have also received relatively little academic attention. Their role is to bring specialist knowledge to bear in selecting the particular securities to include in a portfolio; they normally limit their purchases to the area (geographic, sectoral, or both) in which they have declared an intention to invest and on which they claim specialist knowledge. Asset managers constitute the bulk of what is referred to as the buy side of the capital market.

A final element in the system of financial intermediation is the investment banks. Nowadays investment banks are allowed also to carry out commercial banking functions in a single institution and therefore tend to be financial supermarkets. An investment bank as it was organized before 1998 did some investing on its own account, some asset managing on behalf of its private clients (the polite euphemism for those who have more money than they know what to do with), trading, underwriting, packaging mortgages or credit card debt and issuing the marketable bonds that they back, mergers and acquisitions, and so on. Perhaps their most important role in intermediating funds from savers to investors was underwriting, that is, helping the ultimate borrowers issue marketable securities (bonds and equities) and placing these with the asset managers. Investment banks acting this way constitute the sell side of the capital market. They are also active on the buy side, investing both on behalf of their private clients and on their own account by their proprietary trading desks, which act pretty much like hedge funds in ferreting out market anomalies and good bets that they judge to offer the prospect of a high rate of return.

One additional distinction is worth noting. Most financial intermediaries, including banks and many asset managers, are organized as profit-making corporations, run for the benefit of their shareholders. A part of the industry, however, is run by trustees on behalf of the clients who make the investments. This part includes the endowments and foundations and also some life insurance companies and pension funds. (Until recently some investment banks were still organized as partnerships, but this is now uncommon.)

Problems

Creditors in the capital markets thus involve a wide array of actors. Some of these are hedge funds and the proprietary trading desks of banks, which may hold long- or short-term assets but in any event frequently do not hold them for very long; others are, or at least were, much more likely to be patient holders. In particular, insurance companies and pension funds issue long-term liabilities with a market value related to the value of their portfolios of assets. Logic therefore says that they can afford to buy and hold long-term assets based on their appraisal of the long-run risk-return trade-off or else place funds with portfolio managers who invest on that basis. Having many such lenders in the capital markets is attractive to borrowers because it allows them to make real investments with an eye to the long term and ride out short-term difficulties by borrowing more rather than liquidating their investments. In particular, such lenders are attractive from the standpoint of emerging markets, which get a chance to borrow without the ever-present threat of a crisis prompted by attempts to run before everyone else has done so.

Unfortunately the asset management business suffers from pervasive principal-agent problems. The ultimate principals, the wealth owners, want a good combination of return and risk. Tastes will differ as regards willingness to bear risk, but everyone wants to be on the risk-return frontier, and individual investors can give some idea of how much risk (and what type of risk, e.g., regarding surprises in real or nominal returns) they are willing to bear.

For several reasons, the agents—the various types of financial intermediaries and fund managers—may find their interests conflicting with those of their principals. To begin with, the agents have a direct interest in being generously rewarded for their professional activities, with rewards that come out of the pockets of their principals to the extent that their remuneration is not necessary to induce their level of performance. Agents who are not particularly talented or industrious obviously have an interest in concealing that fact from their principals so that they get rewarded as though they were particularly meritorious. Furthermore, the agents may be able to profit by diverting investment into activities where their friends can earn rents, at the expense of the returns that the investors can expect to receive. Investment banks, for example, make money out of debt restructurings and may therefore discourage the creditor forbearance that might enable an illiquid debtor to overcome its difficulties in a way that is in the collective interest of the creditors. At times the abuses have been egregious: A particularly notorious example concerns the ways in which Kohlberg Kravis Roberts ripped off their clients during the years of excess in the late 1980s and early 1990s (documented by David Swensen 2000).

Attempts have been made to address these pervasive problems by fashioning appropriate incentive structures. Two are of key importance. The first is legal: The trustees and directors of many of these asset management organizations are defined as having fiduciary responsibilities.[3] That

---

3. Hedge funds do not have fiduciary responsibilities; they invest only sums deposited by those assumed to be able to look after themselves, like rich individuals, and are therefore completely unregulated apart from rules intended to prevent fraud.

is, they are placed under a legal obligation to act prudently to further the interests of those who place money with them, the principal, rather than to pursue their own financial interest. Regulations may then specify further what is and is not to be regarded as prudent; for example, regulations may restrain an insurance company from holding bonds below investment grade or from holding foreign bonds. The alternative approach is known as the prudent-man rule: A fiduciary is permitted to make an investment that is in itself risky if the expected return is judged high enough to justify the level of risk and if the overall portfolio achieves a sufficiently low level of risk.

It is difficult to be certain that a fiduciary is indeed fulfilling its responsibilities because of another pervasive problem that distinguishes the financial markets from the classic perfect market: asymmetric information. The asymmetric information problem will be especially acute if the fiduciary follows a prudent-man rule instead of abiding by a set of arbitrary ratios, which may not result in good investments but do at least provide an easily policed constraint on opportunistic behavior. A contrarian investment policy—seeking to profit from market fads by buying what is temporarily unpopular and selling what is currently popular—is particularly liable to result in losses when the agent's peers are doing well and, thus, to make the fiduciary inappropriately vulnerable to criticism for inadequate performance.

The other key incentive structure intended to respond to the potential gulf between the interests of principals and agents consists of the remuneration structure of the agents, which is intended to align their personal incentives with the welfare of their principals. The standard practice is to pay the agent a base salary that is augmented by the possibility of earning a substantial bonus for superior performance. The base salary is intended to secure a reasonable standard of living for a manager even for a performance that is only normal, and the bonus pays a part of the benefit that would accrue to the agent's principal if the returns are exceptional, thus providing the agent with an incentive to make an effort to achieve such exceptional returns. The bonus is normally based on the extent to which the portfolio that is managed achieves a higher return than the norm for the asset class in which the investment is made, as measured by the index for that asset class. Such indices (for example, the S&P 500 for the US stock market or the EMBI for emerging-market bonds) now exist for all the major asset classes and for many subclasses.[4] The normal practice is for

---

4. The traditional (as opposed to alternative) asset classes considered by Swensen (2000, 159) are long-term US Treasuries, US Treasuries, AAA industrial bonds, mortgage-backed securities, high-yield bonds, emerging-market debt, large-cap US stocks, developed-country foreign stocks, all-cap US stocks, emerging-market stocks, and small-cap US stocks. Swensen emphasizes that asset classes change over time, reflecting changes in the economy, and even at any one point in time a different classification would have been possible.

mutual funds to give quarterly bonuses based on comparison with the chosen index and for pension funds to give bonuses on an annual basis.

The problem with this solution is that the time frame over which bonuses are defined may not be long enough to permit a contrarian investment policy to bear fruit. If bonuses were paid annually and fads lasted only a few months, the bonus system might indeed give a manager the right incentives. But if bonuses are paid on an annual basis (or, worse, if they are paid every three months) while fads can last for years at a time, a totally responsible investment manager who makes long-term contrarian bets can forgo bonuses most of the time. Worse still, the manager may risk getting fired for falling significantly behind the index for a period shorter than a fad can last. The bonus system is an attempt to respond to the very real problem of making sure that managers act in the interest of their principals, but it can provide an incentive for managers to make sure that they do not depart far from the index, a pattern of behavior that can in turn amplify and prolong fads and undermine market efficiency by contributing to herd behavior.

This is presumably a major part of the explanation for the transformation in the financial system that is noted by Henry Kaufman (2000). He argues that in former times most financial institutions operated with a long time horizon, holding assets that they had bought for the long term. In recent years, however, the search to maximize short-run returns in every quarter, which used to be limited to hedge funds and the proprietary desks of the investment banks, has become generalized to the whole of the financial markets, leaving few contrarian or patient investors. This is clearly bad for the borrowers, but there is another issue as well.

Is Short-Termism Good for Creditors?

It is tautological that the long-run return to the lender will be maximized if the short-run return is maximized in every period. Nevertheless, it does not follow that the right way to maximize the long-run return is to seek to maximize the return in every short-run period. The reason is that this creates a danger of precluding a contrarian investment strategy (of buying something when its price falls, when it is most likely to be available at a bargain price). Some contrarian investors, like David Swensen (2000), who has managed the Yale portfolio, have done their principals proud. The principle he used was to decide on the basis of long-run criteria a target allocation of his portfolio among asset classes, which meant that a fall in the price of a class required him to buy more of those assets in order to hold constant the percentage of the portfolio held in that asset class. The contrarian investment strategy was thus built-in and, in practice, yielded richer returns than the constant chase to maximize short-run returns, with the danger of being carried along for too long on fads.

A particularly talented portfolio manager may be able to use personal skills to achieve superior returns, at least as long as the manager's principal is not afraid of risk. That is presumably the reason for the success of the hedge funds: Some people with superior skills may need a regular investment test and reward to motivate them to outperform their peers. But the typical quarterly performance–chaser almost by definition cannot outperform the market, in which case it is not clear why investors should prefer those actively managed funds to indexed funds that give similar returns and incur fewer transaction costs. An increasing number of investors seem to have concluded just that, to judge by the increasing popularity of indexed funds.

Hence, one might think that the way to make the capital markets more friendly to emerging-market borrowers would be to scrap or modify the link of the remuneration of asset managers to market performance. However strongly an asset manager may believe a security to be misvalued by the market, that manager simply cannot afford to follow personal convictions if the manager believes the crowd is going to perpetuate its error for any length of time. That is the way to risk not only a bonus but even the job. Professional prudence dictates not straying too far from the benchmark, that is, not defying the herd. Why not simply prohibit bonuses?

Doubtless the lawyers would have a field day devising ways around any such prohibition if it were to be imposed, but an even more basic reason is that the bonus responds to a very real problem—that of aligning the interests of principals and their agents. How about the possibility of modifying the bonus formula instead? During my research as background for this study, I talked to a number of firms, some of which were seeking alternatives because they recognized a problem with current practices. I talked to one company that was experimenting with alternative formulas by using three-year as well as one-year performance and a cap on the bonus if the manager beat the benchmark by more than 250 basis points, on the argument that this would discourage gambling behavior. A pension fund said that it specifically sought managers who did not make a practice of hugging the benchmark. One manager said that his organization did not make use of bonuses at all. Most firms can see a problem, but it is one they do not know how to deal with: Rejecting the use of the benchmark would mean they would have no way to evaluate managers at all.

Because the problem is that the bonus design provides an incentive to follow the herd in the short run without paying proper attention to the likely long-run consequences of where the herd is heading, a natural possibility would be to introduce longer-run performance into the design. Suppose, for example, that a manager were paid a quarterly or annual bonus only after a delay. To be specific, suppose that a manager were to be paid the bonus for performance in 2004 after five years, in 2009, only if subsequent events had not established that the investment strategy being pursued was flawed. This would provide a very concrete incentive to assess the longer-term sustainability of the manager's strategy, and it would not be difficult to use tax policy to encourage all asset management organizations to revise their remuneration practices in this way. One could provide that bonuses paid more promptly or without appropriate conditionality would not count as an expense that the employer was entitled to deduct from revenue in calculating taxable profit.

Such an approach would be relatively easy if asset managers stayed in the same job for their whole careers; they would receive their year 2004 bonus in due course provided that the portfolios they were managing had not performed worse than some agreed standard in the succeeding five years.[5] This approach unfortunately runs into difficulties when a manager quits. One surely would not want to give an artificial incentive to accelerated turnover of managers by paying out the bonus unconditionally to any manager who quit the job. Could one notionally freeze the portfolio as it was on the leaving date and apply the agreed test to that hypothetical portfolio? Because managers change their portfolios all the time, that would hardly seem just. Would one look at the performance achieved by the manager's successor and assume that the departing manager's policy would have been the same? If that is a good assumption, one has to have doubts as to whether it was worth hiring or firing one or the other manager. Would one require the departing manager to continue managing a hypothetical portfolio for the succeeding five years to establish that the manager could have achieved the hurdle level of performance? That would be wasteful and appears quite unrealistic. In short, there seems no remotely satisfactory solution. But is that really sufficient reason to abandon the attempt to introduce a concern for longer-term results into the incentives facing asset managers?

An alternative approach would involve more radical change in the way the industry functions, with trustees taking a bigger part of the burden on themselves. Instead of hiring managers to make the critical decisions and seeking to blame those managers when things go wrong, trustees could themselves decide to buy and hold for the long term. Or they could decide that a certain proportion of their portfolios was going to be invested in an asset class like emerging-market bonds and then hire a manager to look after it for 5 or 10 years, with a bonus to be determined only at the end of that period on the basis of cumulative performance over the whole period. They might even experiment with assigning a portfolio to a manager for a 10-year period and then rely on the manager's sense of professional responsibility to act in the best long-term

---

5. One possible standard would be that the portfolio had never fallen more than a certain percentage, say 20 percent, below its value at the end of the reference year over the succeeding five years. Another might be that its value at the end of the five-year period was at least as great as its value on the reference date.

interest of the principals. After all, some people find that a professional challenge provides sufficient motivation for exceptional effort, without a need for monetary incentives.

One can hope that such practices as these will be adopted in some companies and may even spread. However, I was unable to persuade myself that they provide a basis for a program that could be instituted by public policy. In the next two chapters we turn to examine proposals that would more readily lend themselves to policy initiatives.

6

What Creditors Could Do

Bad lending decisions should be attributed just as much of a role in creating financial crises as rash borrowing decisions. Accordingly, an examination of what can be done to stabilize the boom-bust cycle needs to look at the possibilities of action on the part of creditors as well as debtors. Indeed, when this project was started, my idea was to see whether the problem could be cured entirely from the side of the lenders. In the end, I concluded that this was just not feasible, partly because there seems no way of escaping from remunerating asset managers on the basis of the short-run performance of the portfolios they manage, but that certainly does not mean that I would want to go to the other extreme and put all the onus of avoiding future crises on reforms by the borrowers, as discussions in the official sector have for the most part tended to do. This chapter is therefore devoted to examining the scope for reforms on the part of lenders; the next chapter turns to the borrowers.

What actions might encourage equity flows and might make them more stable? These prove to be distinctly limited: Desirable as equity flows may be, there is not a lot that governments can do to stimulate further the flows of this type to emerging markets. The chapter then turns to two generic ideas for reducing the crisis potential from flows involving the purchase of fixed-income assets. This is followed by looking separately at proposals for reforming the lending of the multilateral development banks (MDBs), of the commercial banks, and of the private bond markets.

Equity

It has already been argued in this study (chapter 4) and elsewhere (e.g., Rogoff 1999) that there are good reasons, especially in terms of risk sharing, for desiring a shift of capital flows from loans to equity. From the standpoint of vulnerability to capital flow reversal, however, most analysts would differentiate sharply between the two forms of equity capital—FDI and portfolio investment. Multinationals will surely try to profit from any one-way bets that may be presented to them by misguided exchange rate policies by shifting their working capital around, and having investments in a country may stimulate operations that appear to them hedging while similar operations in the absence of investment might have been precluded as obviously speculative. Nevertheless, multinationals will not shift their fixed investments in any significant way in response to short-run fears of crisis, and covering is likely to be modest in comparison with the volume of investment. Individual portfolio investors, in contrast, believe they have the possibility of liquidating their investments, and many of them make a conscious effort to enhance their returns by judicious market timing. As noted in chapter 4, the preponderance of the evidence points to the conclusion that portfolio investors are more fickle than domestic investors in similar assets, and, therefore, they tend to magnify booms and busts.

Nowadays no developed country maintains important restrictions on the ability of its firms to invest abroad; therefore, there is little of first-order importance that can be done to encourage FDI. However, countries have quite a few minor ways in which they can stimulate appropriate foreign investments by their companies. The scorecard used in the investment component of the 2005 Commitment to Development Index of the Center for Global Development provides an excellent guide. The index rewards countries that are members of multilateral investment insurance agencies, notably the Multilateral Investment Guarantee Agency. It also rewards countries for having a national insurance agency but penalizes them if that agency makes no attempt to monitor standards with regard to the environment, labor, or human rights; if investors in certain sectors are ineligible for cover; if that insurance agency uses national economic interest tests that are at the expense of the host country; if that agency covers inefficient import substitution projects; or if it restricts eligibility to firms majority-owned by its nationals. The index also rewards countries for preventing double taxation, for example, if they sign tax-sparing agreements, and the index penalizes them if they prevent their investors from benefiting from developing country tax incentives. It rewards them for subscribing to and implementing the OECD antibribery convention and for participating in the Extractive Industries Transparency Initiative workshop. It also rewards them if they provide official assistance in identifying investment opportunities or in developing local investment promotion agencies.

In other words, there are quite a few things, albeit not high-profile actions, that developed countries can do to encourage an enlightened form of FDI by their firms in developing countries.

Encouraging FDI but not foreign portfolio investment would create a bias toward foreign firms as suppliers to markets in emerging countries because it would deny any route for foreign equity investors to supply capital to domestic firms. Even if one is not quite so convinced that foreign portfolio investment is a boon for emerging markets as most people now agree FDI to be, it seems reasonable to think that portfolio investment should be encouraged rather than the converse.

Here the main battle has already been won. For a long time most of the big countries of continental Europe had regulations, based on the old-fashioned principle that the way to safeguard investors is to prevent investment in anything that is not super-safe, that precluded their pension funds investing in emerging markets. However, after much argument, the European Union's Financial Services Action Plan provided an agreed legal framework for cross-border investments that firmly embeds the prudent-man principle as the basis for the regulation of pension funds and strictly curbs the restrictions that member states may impose. Thus, all pension funds must be allowed to invest at least 70 percent of their portfolio in shares, and they must be allowed to hold at least 30 percent of their portfolio in non-euro assets. Once this reform has entered into force, it will be difficult to argue that there are any serious restraints on portfolio investment in emerging markets on the part of EU members. In fact, the main constraints on such investments will be those maintained in— not by—the United States, where a number of individual states impose old-fashioned regulations that preclude or limit foreign investment by pension funds or insurance companies based in those states (especially by the pension funds of state agencies).

If there is not much more to be done in terms of liberalizing portfolio equity investment by industrial countries, is there something that could be done to reduce its volatility? For example, when portfolio investment in emerging markets first started, much of it took place through the medium of closed-end investment funds.[1] Because these closed-end funds are typically unable to switch their funds out of a country even if the market has begun to suspect that the country may be heading for a crisis, why not revive them? This is in fact most unlikely: Most closed-end funds were

---

1. A closed-end fund is one where the money placed in the fund remains invested in the recipient country irrespective of the desire of the investors to liquidate their holdings. The effect of a net desire to liquidate holdings is therefore to depress the price of the fund's shares on the market of the capital-exporting country rather than to cause a sale of shares on the market of the capital-importing country. (The fund's managers retain the right to change the *composition* of the fund's assets, but the assets remain in the country that the fund advertised that it planned to invest in.)

created because that was the only way that a number of emerging markets were at first prepared to allow foreign portfolio equity investment. To reimpose the restrictions that have subsequently been lifted so as to re-create the incentive to run closed-end funds would risk jeopardizing the goodwill of the financial community, even if it were administratively practical. Now that emerging markets have opened up to other forms of foreign investment, investors have no incentive to hold closed-end funds, which usually trade at a significant discount to the value of the assets held by the fund. This is believed to be because once it has been set up, a closed-end fund has a monopoly on the management of those assets and can therefore charge higher management fees than the competitive rate. Because investors know they have no way of bringing competitive pressure to bear, they simply have to accept a lower return on the assets held by the fund, for which reason they pay a lower price to purchase those assets.[2]

Nowadays closed-end funds may almost have disappeared, but an analogous distinction still exists between dedicated and crossover investors. Dedicated investors are those funds that restrict their investments to one geographical region (usually broader than a country—typically Asia, Latin America, or even emerging markets) or possibly one sector; crossover investors switch their funds between emerging markets and any other markets. During the Asian crisis, it was mainly the crossover investors who sold out because they were anxious to avoid being found holding tainted assets; the dedicated investors held fast, relatively secure in the knowledge that their purchasers knew what they were buying and expected some volatility as the price of the good returns they anticipated in the longer run. Hence, investors in emerging markets mainly constituted dedicated investors by the end of the crisis.

The emerging-market recovery of 2003–04 was fueled by a return of the crossover investors as well as by a surge of new money into the dedicated funds, so that now the crossover investors are reputed to be again a major element in the picture. Differential taxation would seem about the only handle through which public policy might conceivably be able to operate and reward the dedicated investors as against the crossovers. The problem is that, because there is no legal distinction between dedicated and crossover investors, this would require a public body that distinguished the deserving dedicated investors from the undeserving crossover ones and that made sure that the former group did not violate the rules that had led to their classification as dedicated investors. Perhaps it is better to accept a degree of volatility in equity prices and rely on the existence of

---

2. Part of the academic literature (Lee, Shleifer, and Thaler 1990) questions this explanation, but that is academic indeed as long as this explanation is widely believed in the markets, which seems to be the case.

investors who understand that the logic of contrarian investing favors the dedicated funds rather than the crossovers.

All Fixed-Interest Lenders

Two proposals could potentially apply to all nonequity investments. One is intended to achieve a shift in the currency of denomination of loan contracts so that, instead of being written in the currencies of the lenders (notably in the dollar), they are denominated in the domestic currency of the borrower. The other proposal is intended to allow borrowers a bit of breathing space in the event of a crisis, in the hope that they would be able to regain confidence and resume normal business if given a little extra time.

The problem of currency mismatches arises when the currency of a borrowing country is devalued against the currency in which many loan contracts are written. A major part of the problem in East Asia in 1997 was that exchange rate crises provoked major devaluations, which then meant that the many domestic agents who had borrowed in dollars—either banks or their borrowers—were exposed to drastic increases in the value of their liabilities without any compensating increase in the value of their assets. These currency mismatches thus provoked, or at the very least worsened, financial crises. The same happened in Argentina in 2001, and the escalation of the value of much of the public debt that was indexed to the dollar was an important factor behind the market panic in Brazil in 2002.

Morris Goldstein and Philip Turner (2004) analyze the problem of currency mismatches in depth. Their proposed solutions focus largely on actions by emerging economies and will therefore be considered in chapter 7. However, they also suggest that "the IMF should publish regularly data on currency mismatches at the economywide and sectoral levels and should draw attention to those mismatches regarded as excessive." This would at least act as a stimulus to emerging-market governments in taking the sort of actions they suggest to discourage mismatching.

An altogether more drastic solution was proposed by Anne Krueger (2000), now (though not when she advanced the proposal) the first deputy managing director of the IMF. She suggested that developed countries should lend to emerging markets only in their own currencies. A whole literature (e.g., Eichengreen and Hausmann 2003) asserts, although it has never tried to prove, this to be impossible because the countries suffer from "original sin," which means that foreign investors would refuse to lend by buying assets denominated in the borrower's own currencies. Krueger suggested that investors nonetheless be deprived of the alternative of lending in their own currencies, which would end such lending if the original-sin people are right but would transform it to a more benign form if they are wrong (box 6.1).

Box 6.1 Original sin

Ricardo Hausmann originally termed an inability to borrow abroad in domestic currency "original sin." The term suggested that countries borrow abroad by issuing liabilities denominated in foreign currencies because they have no choice; it is the only way that foreigners will lend to them. Hausmann has used this term in a series of papers he has written in association with Barry Eichengreen and in some cases with Ugo Panizza; more recently a number of other authors, including some like Goldstein and Turner (2004) who are sharply critical of the Eichengreen-Hausmann policy proposals, have used the term.

A frequent consequence of original sin, which means borrowing abroad in foreign currency, is the creation of a currency mismatch, a state in which assets and liabilities are denominated in different currencies. Thus, an Indonesian corporation that borrowed abroad in dollars but sold at home in rupiahs would acquire a currency mismatch as a consequence of original sin. But the two phenomena are conceptually distinct. If the Indonesian firm sold abroad in dollars, its debt obligations would be hedged by its foreign exchange earnings, and so original sin would not create a currency mismatch. Conversely, an Argentinean borrower who earned pesos and whose mortgage from a local bank was denominated in dollars (pre-2001) would have a currency mismatch without any foreign borrowing being involved.

Eichengreen and Hausmann have also used the term "domestic original sin" to refer to the supposed inability to issue long-term, fixed-rate debt in domestic currency. At one time Eichengreen and Hausmann even argued that an inability to borrow abroad in domestic currency and to borrow long-term at home in domestic currency on fixed-rate terms were two aspects of the same phenomenon, but their more recent work recognizes that these are two distinct problems.

Another related concept that has been introduced in recent work by Reinhart, Rogoff, and Savastano (2003) is "debt intolerance," meaning an inability to carry a high volume of debt without running into a debt crisis. The term is again quixotic inasmuch as it suggests that it is the debtor that refuses to countenance a high level of debt, whereas the analysis says that, because of suspicions in the capital market, countries with a history of reneging on their debt find that the terms become adverse when their debt is still relatively modest. Either original sin, currency mismatches, or domestic original sin may contribute to debt intolerance, but they are again distinct phenomena.

(box continues next page)

Krueger (2000) identified two alternative ways in which a legal requirement to denominate a loan in the borrower's own currency might be created. One would involve action on the part of the borrowing countries, and discussion of it is therefore deferred to chapter 7. Krueger's other way of forcing financial institutions to lend in the borrower's currency envisaged action on the part of the lending countries. They would "pass and enforce legislation requiring their financial institutions to accept liabilities [presumably she meant assets] abroad only in local currencies, and to hedge foreign-exchange risks in international markets." It is not clear whether this would completely eliminate the problem of currency mis-

Box 6.1 *(continued)*

Why is it a problem if a country borrows abroad in some other country's currency? Because it makes for instability when done by a debtor country. When a debtor country is forced to devalue, it finds that the value of its debts in terms of its own currency has suddenly increased, thus magnifying its problems. Note that this is still true even if the microeconomic agent that had borrowed abroad was covered because it was an exporter; had it borrowed in domestic currency instead, the devaluation would have reduced the foreign currency value of its debts, easing the national situation at what one assumes to be a difficult time. Conversely, when a currency appreciates, that is usually a time when a country is in a good situation to take on an additional burden; for a debtor country that has borrowed abroad in foreign currency, this is a time when the country suddenly finds its burden is eased. To them that hath shall be given.

Note that these effects work in reverse for creditor countries: A devaluation increases the (domestic currency) value of a creditor country's assets if these were invoiced in foreign currency, helping the creditor country's adjustment; and a revaluation reduces the domestic currency value of its foreign currency denominated assets, meaning it gets less help when it does not specially need help anyway.

Hence, both debtor and creditor countries can benefit if assets are denominated in the currency of the debtor. At least, that would be the case if debtors could be relied upon not to inflate away their debts. So long as creditors are not totally convinced that borrowers have grown out of such temptations, prudence will suggest that they should lend in the debtor's currency only if their asset is inflation indexed.

Eichengreen and Hausmann have provided abundant evidence that original sin is widespread, but there is no convincing evidence that it is inevitable. There are emerging market countries—most conspicuously South Africa—that borrow in their own currency. Growth is rapid in domestic bond markets in emerging markets that issue bonds that are denominated predominantly in domestic currency. Foreign investors buy some of these bonds, thus accepting exposure to currency risk in countries that are supposedly afflicted by original sin. Indeed, some investment banks run funds consisting exclusively of the local currency denominated bonds of emerging markets. Shortly before this study went to press there was a report that the Banco do Brasil had sold domestic currency denominated bonds in the international market, where they were readily sold. Although it should certainly be an objective of policy to largely rid the world of foreign currency denominated borrowing, to blame such borrowing on original sin is silly.

matches or simply transfer it within the country because someone has to take the other side of the foreign-exchange hedge, and it is only if that someone were a foreigner that the problem would be eliminated. But even if a national were to take the hedge, it would hopefully be someone in a better position to carry the risk (such as an exporter that earns income denominated in foreign currency).

Krueger relied on developed-country bank supervisors to enforce the provision that foreign assets be denominated only in local currencies. This would constrain financial institutions that are dependent on their supervisors, like banks, but might not apply to bonds or certificates of deposit sold by emerging-market issuers to foreign mutual funds, pension funds, insurance companies, or other financial intermediaries. It might thus be difficult to legislate a complete abandonment of foreign currency borrowing (even if the original-sin people are wrong), but even a switch to domestic currency lending by banks might make the system much less crisis prone.

The other proposal that is intended to cover all loans (including bonds) addresses the problem of a run. This proposal is due to Buiter and Sibert (1999, 231–32), who suggested including what they called a universal debt rollover option with a penalty (UDROP) in all foreign currency obligations (including bonds, loans, and options).

> All foreign-currency IOUs must have a rollover option attached to them. This includes private and sovereign, long-term and short-term, marketable and nonmarketable, negotiable and non-negotiable debt, including overdrafts, credit lines, and contingent claims. . . . All borrowers, public and private, must be given the option. . . .
>
> The option would entitle the borrower, at his sole discretion, to extend maturing debt for a specified period (say three or six months) at a penalty rate. The borrower would be entitled to the rollover only if the debt in question had been serviced in full, barring the final repayment. . . .
>
> We expect the penalty spread and other features of the rollover contract to be negotiated between debtors and creditors, rather than decreed by a government or international body.

The purpose of the proposal is to relieve the liquidity pressures that build up in crisis situations. Buiter and Sibert emphasize that their scheme is intended only to help an otherwise solvent borrower that is unable to roll over its foreign currency debt because of a liquidity crisis. And it would surely be attractive if one could feel confident that liquidity crises would be resolved within three or six months.[3]

Unfortunately that would seem likely only when liquidity crises are pure panics that are resolved merely by the passage of time. But liquidity crises normally develop when creditors begin to harbor doubts about the ability of debtors to service their debt on the contractually agreed terms, and they end only when those doubts are resolved. The crucial question is why a three-month (or a six-month) delay without any restructuring of debt obligations beyond that point should allay such doubts: The presumption has to be that the debtor's condition will be essentially the same at that time as it was when the UDROP was exercised, which implies that all a UDROP would accomplish would be to delay the crisis.

---

3. There are at least two ways, however, in which the intent of the proposal could be negated. One would be by denominating international loans in the currency of the borrower, which would at least have the merit of eliminating original sin. The other would be by the borrower and lender contracting for the rollover to be exercised at a prohibitive interest rate, to which the borrower might agree if it wished to demonstrate to the lender that it had no intention of exercising the option—but which would then leave the borrower high and dry if in the end it encountered a crisis.

Perhaps an amended version of the UDROP proposal could play a more strategic role if it were accepted that an extension of loan maturities was a normal part of the solution to a liquidity crisis. In general, an extension of much more than six months seems likely to be needed in order to resolve a crisis; recall that Korea and its bank creditors negotiated a three-year extension of maturities at the end of 1997. Of course, no one would suggest writing an automatic UDROP of three years; this is a dimension that ought not to be prespecified but instead negotiated between the debtor and a creditor committee ad hoc as and when the rollover option is invoked. Creditors will presumably seek the shortest rollover period that gives assurance of allowing the debtor to restore its liquidity and exit from crisis. But if the creditors are recalcitrant in agreeing to a realistic time frame, it would seem desirable to relieve the debtor of the obligation of paying amortization pro tem. This would need to be approved by some appropriate arbiter, such as the IMF or a specially created ad hoc body. The incentive for the debtor to agree to the shortest realistic period for the rollover is to preserve its standing in the capital markets.

Creditors have reacted adversely to the UDROP idea. If it turns out they are so strongly averse to it as to bring lending to a halt, one might exempt long-term loans above a certain maturity. Trade credits might be allowed to satisfy the requirement by a provision that a given volume of credits revolve over time, on the model of the banks' 1998 agreement with Brazil. But the loans that should not be exempted, no matter how severe the impact on volume, are short-term loans without any trade contract as collateral. It is true that UDROP would add to the risk of short-term lending to a debtor whose medium-term position looks doubtful, but that is the point. Short-termist lenders would find it more difficult to persuade themselves that they can buy short-term assets and then win the race to the exits if things go wrong. The game in which investment bankers advise their clients that it is safe to buy short-term assets from country X because it looks safe enough for the next few months would be undercut. Only investors willing to make a relatively long-term commitment would invest in emerging-market loans, and those are the only investors worth having.

Multilateral Development Banks

A solution to the problem of the currency mismatches that arise from the lending of the MDBs has been advanced by Eichengreen and Hausmann (2003). Although I agree with Goldstein and Turner (2004) that the habit of borrowing in a foreign currency is not so deeply embedded that it makes sense to label it original sin, I also believe that the proposal Eichengreen and Hausmann made to overcome the problem with regard to MDB lending deserves more than the summary dismissal it has received from such influential writers as Goldstein and Turner and Rajan (2004).

The specific proposal of Eichengreen and Hausmann is to have the MDBs borrow in a synthetic unit whose value is determined by a basket of inflation-indexed emerging-market currencies.[4] The World Bank, for example, would sell bonds denominated in this unit to international investors. Eichengreen and Hausmann reason that such a basket would be potentially attractive to investors (of which the proverbial Belgian dentist is the archetypal example) for several reasons. Being indexed, its value could not be inflated away. Being a basket, its value would tend to be more stable than that of individual emerging-market currencies.[5] The basket would be expected to exhibit mild secular appreciation against (for example) the dollar, for two reasons: because it is fully indexed while the dollar is not and because most of the constituent currencies would be of countries that can expect to benefit from the Balassa-Samuelson effect in coming decades.

To cover itself against exchange risk, all that the World Bank would need to do would be to on-lend the borrowed money on an indexed basis in the currencies that constitute the index in the proportions that make up the basket.[6] Because the Bank's lending would be indexed, the borrowing countries would be unable to inflate away their debts. On the other hand, a real depreciation of a country's currency necessitated by a crisis or a need for adjustment would maintain its debt constant in terms of its real (inflation-adjusted) domestic currency but reduce its debt in terms of foreign currencies. Thus, no problems of currency mismatches would arise through borrowing from the MDBs. This is in sharp contrast with the past, when the reluctance of the MDBs to engage in imaginative financial engineering in the lending they offer to their borrowers at times resulted in major financial burdens on the borrowers (see Kapur, Lewis, and Webb 1997, chapter 16). The Bank's real lending rate could, of course, be the same for all borrowers, just as its dollar lending rate is the same for all.

Note that this proposal deals with a part of emerging-market borrowing that would not be reformed by any of the other proposals dealt with in this study. In particular, it is a complement to, rather than a substitute

---

4. Every proposal for financial innovation stimulates skeptics to ask why the market has not already developed the asset that is being advocated. An answer to that rhetorical question, which is based on Borensztein and Mauro (2004), is summarized in the concluding chapter of this study.

5. Eichengreen and Hausmann simulate the behavior of two hypothetical 20-country baskets and show that their volatility against the dollar would have been comparable with that of major international currencies.

6. Presumably the Bank would not be able to secure an exact hedge in this way unless it were constantly changing the composition of the basket in which it borrowed, which would undermine the ability to create a vibrant market in the synthetic unit; however, marginal remaining exposures could be hedged through the financial markets.

for, the reforms in emerging-market borrowing that were advocated by Goldstein and Turner and that are endorsed in chapter 7.

Commercial Banks

After the oil price increase in the 1970s, banks played a major role in intermediating funds to emerging markets in the form of trade credits or, even more important at that time, syndicated loans. As a result, banks were at the heart of the debt crisis of the 1980s. They never regained their role as the dominant lenders during the new boom in capital flows in the 1990s. They nonetheless again became a significant source of funds, though with a much diminished role for medium-term syndicated credits to the public sector and a correspondingly larger role (especially in East Asia) for short-term loans to the private sector, particularly interbank loans. And, as before, it was their flow of funds that turned decisively negative soon after the crisis started and that therefore contributed most acutely to worsening the East Asian crisis.

One reason that bank lending is so volatile is that banks lend in the form of loans that can be liquidated simply by not rolling them over when times turn difficult. Although many of these loans in the 1970s had a medium-term maturity, one of the conclusions that banks drew from the debt crisis was that they would be safer lending only with the traditional short-term tenors, so that they would find it easier to liquidate their positions if events looked threatening. This relies on a fallacy of composition, for although it may be easier for any one bank to liquidate its loans, an attempt by bankers collectively to get out is prone to provoke the very crisis that they are individually seeking to avoid.

The main responsibility for not borrowing in such a dangerous form has to rest with borrowers and will therefore be discussed in chapter 7. Nevertheless, this does not imply that there is nothing the lenders can do. Various authors have in fact suggested several different approaches that the authorities of the lending countries can take in order to make the lending by their banks less problematic.

Perhaps the most familiar idea is that the authorities should withdraw the encouragement they have in the past provided for banks to lend short term by revising the first Basel agreement, which required them to hold less capital against short-term loans of less than a year's maturity. The final version of the new Basel agreement, known as Basel II, will indeed change this requirement, but in the wrong direction! Small banks subject to the standardized approach will still be allowed lower risk weights for short-term interbank loans—defined as those with a maturity of less than three months (Basel I specified one year). At least there is an improvement so far as large (highly rated) banks are concerned: Such banks will be subject to a 20 percent risk weight for all interbank lending regardless of maturity.

The Basel negotiators have worked on the premise that supervisors ought to concern themselves only with the interests of bank depositors. My colleagues Wendy Dobson and Gary Hufbauer (2001) argued that the supervisors of the banks of the main industrial countries should be required to take a broader view of their social obligations. They accordingly looked to a number of changes in the process of bank supervision to ameliorate the problem of volatility in lending to emerging markets. They argued that bank supervisors have the ability and, hence, a responsibility to change the incentive systems that banks face in a way that will dampen the volatility of their lending, which they attribute to the fact that the banks enjoy a publicly provided safety net. This gives banks an incentive to engage in unduly risky behavior, pushing loans—even to risky borrowers—when times are good, in the expectation that the safety net will prevent the worst if they should have difficulty liquidating their loans when times turn bad.

Dobson and Hufbauer welcomed the general thrust of the reforms to bank supervision that are proposed in Basel II, but they suggested a number of modifications designed to make industrial-country bank supervisors contribute to the stability of the system. They argued that risk weights should be higher for loans to particularly risky borrowers, and they identified two groups they would place in that category. One is emerging-market borrowers with weak financial systems. The other is highly leveraged hedge funds. One might add that one of the strengths of Basel II is that an attempt has been made to vary the risk weights applied to corporate borrowers to reflect their differential riskiness.

Echoing a proposal first advanced by staff of the Federal Reserve Board in a different context (Kupiec and O'Brien 1997), Dobson and Hufbauer (2001) also proposed that banks in the nonstandard category, those using internal ratings rather than the standard approach to determine risk weights, should be fined if the risks prove ex post to have been underrated. They urged supervisors to be alert to evidence of herding in the form of a run into emerging-market assets, and they argued that supervisors should tighten capital requirements in an internationally coordinated fashion if they see that happening. They proposed that banks should be allowed—but not compelled—to use subordinated debt to meet a part of their capital requirements, an arrangement that would co-opt the capital markets into helping the supervisors police the banks. Inevitably, they also urged better disclosure and greater transparency. In addition, banks should be encouraged to provide more adequately for future loan losses by requiring the tax authorities to automatically accept loan-loss provisions that have been endorsed by bank regulators rather than allow such provisioning only when the evidence is irrefutable that loans have actually turned bad. Although I have doubts as to whether these changes alone would suffice to curb the past volatility of bank lending, their series of ideas is highly sensible.

An even more radical proposal regarding provisioning for future loan losses has been advanced by Jean-Claude Trichet, now the governor of the European Central Bank and previously governor of the Banque de France, and, more recently, by José Antonio Ocampo (2003). They have proposed that all the industrial-country banks should be expected to adopt the policy of forward-looking provisioning that is required of Spanish banks by their supervisors.[7] Forward-looking provisioning means setting aside provisions not just for loans that are already recognized as being problematic but also for the statistically expected level of future loan losses. The idea is that when an economy enters into recession the banks would already have made significant provisions for the loan losses that would then materialize; therefore they would be unlikely to be forced into lending cutbacks that would further accentuate the recession. Indeed, it is conceivable that it would turn out that their provisions were greater than needed, in which case the banks would actually be in a position to step up lending in a cyclical downturn instead of retrenching, as has been the normal historical experience. Even if banks maintain their traditional policy of cutting and running when times turn tough, the innovation would at least serve to restrain the extent to which they could overlend in the good times.

Another proposal is addressed specifically to the tendency of the banks to cut and run when a crisis materializes, especially by not rolling over loans in the interbank market. Henri Bernard and Joseph Bisagnano (1999, 41) suggest "an ex post charge for liability insurance . . . triggered . . . when official assistance is required to resolve a country's financial crisis. . . . Interbank lenders could then be assessed an ex post insurance premium, related to their withdrawals, in other words, a 'haircut'." The expectation of being assessed such a premium (or subjected to an exit tax, to use an alternative terminology) could be helpful insofar as it deterred banks from making short-term loans in the first place or from liquidating their loans in the midst of a crisis. It seems clear, however, that the size of the insurance premium (exit tax) that would be required to resolve a crisis if the banks were not in fact deterred would be uncomfortably large if this were the sole mechanism for reducing contractual payments to what the country could afford to pay.

---

7. José Antonio Ocampo (2003, 236) explains:

> The best-known [case of forward-looking provisioning over the cycle] is Spain, which in December 1999 issued a regulation requiring countercyclical provisions calculated by statistical methods. The main feature of this approach is the estimation of "latent risk" based on past experience over a period long enough to cover at least one business cycle. This generates a dynamic in which provisions build up during economic expansions and are drawn upon during downturns. . . . The major innovation of this system is its explicit recognition that risks are incurred when credits are approved and disbursed, not when they fall due.

In most cases, what will be needed to achieve rapid recovery from a crisis will be a debt reconstruction that stretches maturities rather than the reconstitution of some part of the liquidity that has been lost. This approach may thus be helpful in undermining the confidence of bank lenders that they will win the race to the exits if trouble develops, but it will not necessarily be of much help in resolving a crisis that has already developed.

Bonds

Before the Second World War, long-term bonds provided the principal mechanism for lending to the emerging markets of the day. Today bonds tend to be of shorter maturity and often also contain put options that reduce their effective maturity to the borrower. Several proposals have been discussed for making bonds more friendly to emerging-market borrowers.

The proposal that first attracted attention was the inclusion of collective action clauses in bond contracts.[8] This was proposed by Eichengreen and Portes (1995) and was then taken up by the Rey Report (Group of Ten 1996). When this proposal was first mooted, we heard dire predictions from some of the New York–based lenders, echoed by some of their clients, that any attempt to include such clauses would bring lending to a halt or, at the least, lead to drastic increases in interest rates. Then someone realized that approximately one-third of such bonds, namely most of those signed in London, already included such clauses. Barry Eichengreen and Ashoka Mody (2000a, 2000b) therefore examined whether the inclusion of such clauses had resulted in higher interest rates to the borrowers, as per the prediction. It turned out that the impact was modest and also, interestingly, that the direction of impact depended on the borrower's creditworthiness. Countries with poor credit ratings did indeed have to pay somewhat more to borrow with the added security of collective action clauses, presumably reflecting lender concern that a lack of willingness to pay might lead borrowers to abuse the clauses even when they would have been able to pay. Countries with good credit ratings actually paid marginally less, presumably reflecting lender recognition that the clauses would reduce the cost of restructuring debt (and the possible interruption in debt service payments while this happened) in the remote contingency that the countries should encounter an inability to pay so that restructuring proved necessary.

Eventually the lawyers found a way of reconstructing bonds issued under New York law, even without collective action clauses (Buchheit and Gulati 2000). The key was to accompany the offer to swap old bonds for

---

8. This is the term given collectively to clauses allowing a bondholders' meeting to be convened to consider a debt reconstruction, rules allowing interest and amortization terms to be modified by a qualified majority of bondholders, sharing clauses, etc.

the new bonds that contain the revised payment terms with proposals to amend the nonpayment clauses of the old bonds in ways that make these much less attractive and impede any holdout bondholders from successfully litigating to demand continued or accelerated payment. Examples of amendments might include old bonds being delisted, the waiver of sovereign immunity being withdrawn, and negative pledge protection being removed. None of these requires the unanimity that prevents revision of the payments clauses. Because these disfiguring amendments to the terms of the old bonds are adopted simultaneously with bondholders exchanging their old bonds for the new debt instruments, they are known as exit consents. Exit consents were used in restructuring junk bonds in the 1980s, but the first time the technique was used to restructure sovereign bonds was in Ecuador in 1999. Exit consents have one great advantage over collective action clauses: They can be used to deal with the stock of old bonds rather than simply allow today's new issues to be restructured in the future. They also have one great disadvantage: They do not give total protection against the threat of litigation by holdouts.

For a while it looked as though countries that needed to restructure their debt were going to have to rely indefinitely on exit consents. But then Anne Krueger (in a speech at the National Economists Club, Washington, November 26, 2001) proposed the creation of a sovereign debt restructuring mechanism (SDRM) in the IMF, and, presto, the far-sighted lenders who had been vigorously opposing collective action clauses decided that they were a lesser evil and would be worth endorsing in order to fend off the threat of the SDRM. All of a sudden the lenders began encouraging issuers to insert collective action clauses in the contracts of new bonds, and the borrowers were only too happy to oblige. In this respect, reform has already happened.

Bond borrowing is more useful to emerging markets if the bonds are long term because that means there is less scope for the lender to cut and run in difficult times. One way that nowadays many bonds give scope for cutting and running is by the inclusion of put options. Korea found in late 1997 that many of its creditors chose to exercise their put options, which gave them the right to demand the early return of their money. This meant that Korea faced an additional call on its reserves at the very worst time. A five-year bond with a put option exercisable in six months' time is not really a five-year bond at all; from an economic standpoint it is a short-term, six-month bond with a rollover provision if the lender consents. It should be counted as such in the statistics. Accurately reporting it as such would force both the borrowers and their national authorities to recognize the risks that are being taken. One would expect that this would diminish the attractiveness of agreeing to the inclusion of put options in bond contracts and, hence, lengthen the effective maturity of bonds.

Regulations require that insurance companies registered in a number of states in the United States may hold only investment-grade bonds. This is a legacy from the days when fiduciary requirements were enforced by limiting what the fiduciary was entitled to hold instead of holding fiduciaries to the prudent-man standard. It is not clear that it any longer makes sense: One can surely argue that insurance companies should be allowed to decide for themselves what is in the interest of their clients, subject to supervision by the insurance regulators who make sure that the overall investment policies of the insurance companies do indeed safeguard the interests of their principals.

What makes even less sense is that the fiduciary requirement is specified in terms of what they may hold, not what they may acquire. The difference can be crucial. In late 1997, insurance companies holding Korean bonds were forced by this requirement to sell them in the midst of the market implosion, when credit-rating agencies panicked and suddenly cut Korea's rating to below investment grade. The holders were not allowed to exercise their judgment as to whether Korean bonds remained a good investment (which they certainly were after their price had collapsed). They were forced instead to sell and add to the pressures on Korea, at the cost of their clients. If a requirement such as this is to be retained at all, it needs to be redrafted to limit what insurance companies can buy rather than what they can hold. That would prevent their being forced to sell in response to a credit downgrading, as happened in Korea in late 1997. And that would make bond borrowing more stable.

A Program

Which of these proposals would it make sense to include in an action program designed to make borrowing more stable and thus curb the boom-bust cycle?

In the first place, the system should certainly have a bias in favor of equity rather than fixed-interest lending. No very dramatic actions are available to promote what is essentially an already liberalized policy regime on equity investment; perhaps the main challenge will be to ensure that it remains liberal in the face of the antiglobalization people who think that the way to provide Americans with jobs is to prevent Indians getting hired. A number of secondary actions can help stimulate the flow of FDI, as reviewed above. In addition, a number of US states can liberalize regulations that still prevent pension funds and insurance companies based in those states from investing in emerging markets.

I certainly sympathize with the objective of shifting emerging-market borrowing into their own currencies so as to end currency mismatches, and it is now clear that Eichengreen and Hausmann (2003) were wrong in claiming that this would put an end to capital flows from developed to emerging economies. The Goldstein and Turner (2004) suggestion of having the IMF publicize currency mismatches is a minimal step in support of this objective. The more substantive issues are whether the emerging markets should take the actions discussed in the next chapter and whether developed-country law (enforced by their supervisors) should compel the banks and other financial institutions in their jurisdictions to lend in local currencies. Sympathetic as I am to her objective, it seems to me that the Krueger proposal designed to compel local-currency lending goes too far. There are after all some countries where no responsible bank would be prepared to lend in the local currency and where a forward market for hedging such lending does not exist (or could seize up exactly when most needed). Yet the banks probably ought not to be discouraged from all lending (notably providing trade credit) in such countries. Telling banks they must lend in local currency in some countries but not in others would require the authorities to make judgments that (to put it diplomatically) could prove internationally contentious. It would therefore be better if supervisors were told to encourage rather than compel local currency lending and to encourage banks to cover their lending forward; if that is impossible, supervisors should urge banks to be cautious in how much they lend.

One very concrete proposal for tackling the problem of currency mismatches on a significant part of emerging-market borrowing is that advanced by Eichengreen and Hausmann (2003): MDBs would borrow in an indexed basket of emerging-market currencies and on-lend to emerging markets in their own currencies (indexed to their own consumer price indices). This would eliminate the problem of currency mismatching from MDB lending. This is all gain and no loss. It is ridiculous to dismiss it because one disagrees with parts of the Eichengreen-Hausmann analysis.

This chapter reviewed two proposals designed to limit the ability of investors to cut and run when a crisis materializes. The more ambitious is the Buiter-Sibert (1999) UDROP proposal for including a rollover option at a prespecified penalty interest rate. This seems unlikely as it stands to accomplish much, but an amended version of the proposal that provides for flexibility in the length of the rollover would make sense as one element of a new approach to liquidity crises. The principal difficulty is that one would need some way of deciding whether to extend the rollover while negotiations proceed. A borrower that is not negotiating in good faith could see its rollover terminated and thus become subject to such sanctions as default brings. However, to fashion this proposal into something workable would take a study in itself, and so I do not include it in the action program being assembled here.

The less ambitious proposal along these lines is the Bernard-Bisagnano (1999) proposal: Charge banks that have been lending to any country that needs an official bailout an ex post insurance premium—a premium related to the magnitude of their withdrawals in some preceding period. This seems unlikely to contribute much to resolving a crisis, but it might have some value in deterring short-term lending to countries in a questionable medium-term situation. Once again, however, the value of the contribution is too uncertain to justify inclusion in the action agenda.

A range of ideas would seem able to diminish the volatility of lending by the commercial banks. I disregard what seem to me sensible proposals that do not bear directly on the issue at hand, such as the idea of obliging banks to float subordinated debt to meet a part of their capital requirements. Far more directly relevant would be an amplified risk-weighting system for loans to countries with weak financial systems, as proposed by Dobson and Hufbauer (2001), although it does pose a need to authorize some body to pronounce on which countries have weak systems and which do not. Their proposal to penalize (through fines) banks that use the nonstandard approach to assessing risk weights but turn out ex post to have underestimated the risks also seems eminently reasonable.

Perhaps more important are the ideas for encouraging banks to provide more adequately for future loan losses. The minimum that should be done here is adopt the Dobson-Hufbauer proposal to require the tax authorities to accept automatically loan-loss provisions that have been endorsed by bank regulators. Better still would be to plump for forward-looking provisioning on the Spanish model, as proposed by Jean-Claude Trichet and José Antonio Ocampo (2003).

So far as bonds are concerned, it was suggested that their maturity should be calculated by the term until the next put option falls due or the bond matures, whichever is shorter. The purpose is to discourage the put options that reduce the effective maturity of many bonds below their official terms; the reasoning is that other lenders, and supervisors, would not take false assurance from figures that essentially describe a fiction. Another change that is highly desirable is to eliminate the old-fashioned regulations that prevent many insurance companies from holding high-risk, high-yield bonds. The prudent-man principle should be allowed to apply unfettered, with the managers of the insurance company taking full responsibility for purchasing an appropriate portfolio. If that proves too radical for the authorities to contemplate, the least they should do is amend the requirement that insurance companies hold only investment-grade bonds to one that says they may acquire only investment-grade bonds, so as to eliminate the artificial pressure on them to sell existing bond holdings when the rating agencies panic in the middle of a crisis.

Would this agenda suffice to eliminate the boom-bust cycle? Probably not. That is why this study does not end here but has another chapter dealing with the actions that would also be needed on the part of the borrowers.

7

What Debtors Could Do

Having looked at what the creditors could do to stabilize the flow of capital to emerging markets, we turn in this chapter to a more well-explored topic: what the debtors could do. Certainly the vast bulk of the international action up to now has been in reforming the policies of the debtors. They need to have flexible exchange rates, upgrade their bank supervision, arrange to follow the 12 major standards and codes that are posted on the IMF Web site, eliminate crony capitalism, run budget surpluses so as to reduce debt-GDP ratios to 30 percent odd, and more. The advice has been endless.

What has actually been accomplished also provides an impressive contrast with the two actions on the part of the creditors that were identified in chapter 6: the inclusion of collective action clauses in bond contracts that are signed in New York, and the reforms to bank lending weights under Basel II in order to better reflect risk. Most emerging markets (the major exceptions are China, Ecuador, Hong Kong, and Malaysia) now have exchange rates that float, at least in principle. Much progress has been made in upgrading bank supervision and in implementing many of the other standards and codes, which are regularly reviewed by joint IMF–World Bank missions. Fiscal policies are better than they used to be in Latin America and are largely back in order in East Asia. In East Asia, reserves have gone through the roof, as what the analysis reviewed in chapter 3 concluded should be deficit countries in fact chose to run current account surpluses to protect themselves against the danger of another round of crises.

If emerging markets are once again to become significant net capital importers, as theory suggests would be desirable, they will need to feel secure going into debt. In this chapter we ask what they can do to bring this desirable state of affairs into being.[1]

Macroeconomic Policy

Many past borrowing binges that left a legacy of excessive debt, often in mismatched currencies, arose from the pursuit of rash macroeconomic policies. Hence, a first element in encouraging a continuous capital inflow has to be a resolve to avoid such policies in the future. The objective should not be the fastest growth rate that is possible in the short run but, instead, the fastest that can be sustained over the cycle (which will almost certainly be a faster long-run growth rate than would result from maximizing short-run growth and then precipitating a crisis).

Fiscal policy should aim at reducing debt to a level that allows the possibility of fiscal expansion during a recession. In Latin America, it has been argued that this implies a ratio of public debt to GDP of only around 30 percent (Artana, López Murphy, and Navajas 2003). When debt is much higher than this, there is no point in running a big budget deficit because the only way of financing it is through the inflation tax; the country is unable to implement a countercyclical fiscal policy. A low level of debt will in due course reduce the interest rate that has to be paid, so that debt service will fall for two reasons and thus release fiscal resources for spending on the social sectors and investment.

Monetary policy should also be countercyclical. By far the best way of combining an element of countercyclical monetary policy with the maintenance of confidence by the financial markets is by adopting an explicit inflation targeting framework. Experience in Brazil, Chile, and Mexico has by now demonstrated that this is perfectly feasible in emerging markets (Truman 2003).

Exchange rate policy needs to be free of commitments that might preclude prompt depreciation when a crisis threatens. There also needs to be enough movement in the exchange rate to give borrowers an incentive to avoid or at least cover currency mismatches. It is also important to avoid policies that might lead to an overvaluation of the currency because overvaluation creates the conditions in which crisis vulnerability surges. The regime best calculated to achieve all these desiderata simultaneously is managed floating, where the management is informed by a clear view by the authorities of the trend path of the exchange rate. In my view it is also

---

1. For a similar view on many of these issues, which also stresses the importance of prudent macroeconomic policies, careful oversight of the financial system, and willingness to contemplate using limited capital controls (financial breakwaters), see Bryant (2003, chapter 11).

highly desirable that this view should be publicly articulated, as would be required by the reference rate proposal (Williamson 1998), so as to provide a focus for informed public debate.

Bank Supervision

Public supervision of the banking system is needed because banks often receive public support in order to ward off collapse, which presents bankers with the temptation to take too many risks in the pursuit of the high rewards that they expect to keep if the gamble comes off. Regulation and supervision need to aim at countering those temptations by requiring that bankers take decisions that offer reasonable expectations of reward in light of the risks being undertaken. This is typically pursued by regulations intended to ensure banks' solvency:

- establishing minimum capital adequacy ratios;

- securing that questionable loans are written off rather than evergreened;

- preventing bankers from making loans to their friends rather than to borrowers who offer the best risk-return combination; and

- encouraging risk diversification rather than concentration.

Three specific ways of easing the boom-bust cycle could be pursued through appropriate bank regulations. In the first place, bank provisioning could be reformed to require forward-looking provisioning for domestic banks similar to that advocated in chapter 6 for lending by international banks to emerging markets. This would both help to prevent a credit crunch from developing when a cyclical downturn causes an increase in bad loans and make lending less profitable during the boom and therefore make banks less inclined to go out into the international market and borrow more when capital inflows are already excessive.

The second way to ease the boom-bust cycle is by imposing rules that discourage banks from making foreign currency loans, especially to the nontradable sectors. This might go so far as to ban such loans altogether, although a ban might simply push firms into borrowing abroad unless it was complemented by a prohibition on such borrowing. Alternatively, banks might be required to set aside more reserves against such loans. At the very least, they should be required to keep a record of the magnitude of the potential currency mismatches on their books and to report the size of those mismatched positions.

The third action is to curb the temptation the banks themselves may face of incurring unmatched positions by taking foreign currency denominated loans (e.g., from abroad) and then on-lending the funds in local currency. Bank supervisors need to instruct banks that they should maintain a roughly matched position in foreign currencies, and they need to penalize any banks that fail to follow this instruction. Doubtless some would construe this as a form of capital control although it might better be regarded as an act of prudent supervision that could make capital controls proper less necessary.

Bond Market

It is a great advantage to a country to have its own domestic bond market—in which both the government and corporations are able to borrow onshore—in domestic currency. This helps limit the problem of currency mismatching: Even if all foreign borrowing continues to be in foreign currency, domestic financial intermediation is neither restricted to banks nor need involve the use of a foreign currency. A domestic bond market also raises the possibility that foreigners will buy bonds issued in domestic currency, which would permit foreign borrowing without currency mismatching. Another advantage of a bond market is that, in the worst analysis, a borrower can default on its bonds without threatening to plunge the whole financial system into crisis, as happens when a major bank goes bankrupt and may threaten even the payments system. And it is helpful to the banks in extending longer-term loans to have a bond market in which they can hedge their maturity mismatches.

Bond markets in many emerging markets have expanded greatly in recent years, although Goldstein and Turner (2004, 26–27) note that bond markets are still a larger proportion of GDP in developed countries. They also point out that, once the total bond market is considered,

> the share of the bond market denominated in local currency is not that different between emerging economies and industrial countries. In Asian emerging economies, the local currency share of the bond market is 88 percent—higher than the local currency share in Canada (71 percent) and the United Kingdom (74 percent) and identical to the local currency share in the euro area (88 percent). It is in Latin America that the local-currency share of the bond market (47 percent) is significantly lower than elsewhere.

Governments normally play a central role in the development of a bond market. In particular, they need to issue a range of bonds with different maturities in order to provide a yield curve that will provide guidance to the private sector about realistic prices and yields at which to issue corporate securities. Even if a government does not have an acute need to raise funds for itself, it can justify issuing an appropriate range of bonds as an action to support development of an infant market.

Capital Controls

A country that was isolated from the world capital market by a comprehensive and completely effective system of capital controls would be immune to the problems posed by the boom-bust cycle. At the other extreme, a country that has perfect capital mobility has to choose between losing control of income and losing control of the exchange rate (this is the famous "trilemma"). Is it possible to use partial capital controls to achieve some judicious combination, in which a country retains many of the advantages of capital mobility but is also able to conduct a countercyclical policy and prevent the exchange rate going off to extreme values?

Few economists nowadays have much sympathy for the policy of completely proscribing capital movements or for a system in which any capital flow requires administrative approval from some government authority. The objection to a policy of prohibition is that it prevents presumptively beneficial transactions: Even when an agent has a particularly profitable investment possibility or a particularly urgent need to realize an asset, that agent will be denied the possibility of making or selling an investment. The objections to subjecting transactions to a requirement of administrative approval are that it invites corruption and that even a perfectly honest and conscientious official cannot know whether a plea about why a particular transaction should be permitted is completely true or is exaggerated for the purpose of gaining permission.

More market-oriented controls, like the uncompensated reserve requirement (URR) or *encaje* (in Spanish) that was used in the 1990s in Chile and Colombia, simply alter the price of undertaking such transactions and then leave it to the individual agent to decide whether to consummate the transaction. These certainly address the second objection and also largely the first and are, for those reasons, widely preferred. Administrative controls, such as the famous outflow controls imposed by Malaysia in 1998, may nonetheless have a legitimate role in an emergency. A less well-known requirement was that of Singapore, which required foreigners wishing to borrow Singapore dollars to speculate against the currency to ask the permission of the Monetary Authority of Singapore, which unsurprisingly was not very keen on approving such borrowing in 1997.

An extensive literature has debated the effectiveness of the Chilean URR. I have already surveyed most of this literature in Williamson (2000, 37–45). There is very little dispute that the URR was effective in altering the composition of debt and, in fact, led to longer maturities. The question that was debated was whether the URR also had a macroeconomic effect by increasing the Chilean freedom to raise interest rates and diminishing the inflow of capital to Chile. I pointed out in my previous review of this literature that which of those two outcomes would materialize would depend on a policy decision by the Chilean authorities: They might decide to use their increased policy freedom to raise the interest rate, or they might decide to use it to diminish the inflow of capital (or a bit of both). To the extent that they exploited the freedom to pursue one of those objectives, they would be giving up the ability to pursue the other. Hence all the regressions that found the URR to be an insignificant determinant of both the interest rate and the capital inflow did not really prove it to have been ineffective, as critics of the URR have asserted. They could as well be showing that the authorities used their increased freedom in different ways at different times.[2]

My reading of the literature therefore leaves little doubt in my mind that a country such as Chile is able to use a market-friendly capital control in order to increase its policy autonomy and resist an excessive capital inflow.[3] That still leaves several issues outstanding. Perhaps the most important is whether the typical developing country has the administrative capacity to operate a system of market-friendly capital controls. A second is whether other forms of capital control might be preferable. A third is whether there may still be a place for administrative controls in crisis situations. A fourth is whether the effectiveness of controls tends to erode over time. And a fifth is the appropriate pace of capital account liberalization in countries that initially have controls in place.

The question of administrative capacity is not only the most important, but, unfortunately, it is also the one to which the answer is least clear. We know that a number of Asian countries have had, or in some cases still have, effective administrative controls; China, India, Korea, Malaysia, and Singapore are all examples that come readily to mind. But opinion also seems to be that the controls that Brazil attempted to impose in the 1990s were not very effective, being undermined by the sophistication of the financial markets in Brazil as well as by the complexity of the rules and their frequent changes. Most African countries still have tight capital controls that officially prohibit the export of capital, despite which it is widely believed that capital flight has taken place on a scale that is truly massive relative to the size of the economies in question.

Controls that cannot be reasonably effectively enforced are worse than useless: They breed corruption and tempt policymakers into attempting the infeasible. Thus the question of administrative feasibility has to be a

---

2. There were a number of even more extraordinary attacks. Some critics argued that the increased interest rates that Chilean enterprises had to pay constituted a condemnation of the URR, when they were one of its *purposes*. Others argued that the fact that Chile reduced the URR to zero when capital inflows reversed showed that Chile had concluded that it was a mistaken policy, whereas the intent had been to *smooth* the inflow of capital, which *required* that the URR should vary over the cycle.

3. One can argue, as supporters of the URR did, that the rate of the URR needed to be increased again in 1995–96 in order to resist the new surge of capital that hit Chile at that time, but the fact that Chile failed to raise the URR did not prove that it was ineffective.

big issue in deciding whether to use capital controls in a particular country and also in deciding what form of controls should be used. Feasibility of administration also argues in favor of having a control (like a requirement that some transactions go through a dual exchange market) that is permanently in place but (as when the dual rate usually stands at a trivial premium or discount) normally gives little incentive to the private sector to learn to evade.

The second issue is in deciding on the form of capital control. Excluding rules imposed by bank supervisors, which sometimes come close to being capital controls, the options include administrative controls, a URR, a tax on capital inflows or outflows (such as discussed by Zee 1999),[4] and segmentation of some or all capital flows into a parallel market. I have already explained why the first option is undesirable as a regular feature of the system (the emergency use of administrative controls is discussed below).

The second option proved administratively feasible in Chile; the market found enough loopholes to make it necessary repeatedly to amend the rules, but it remained reasonably effective to the end, as demonstrated by the continued denunciation of the *encaje* by those it inconvenienced.

One of the advantages that Howell Zee (1999) claims for the third alternative (which was indeed an alternative to the URR that was offered to those importing capital in Chile) is that it would be administratively simpler. Assuming that it were used to tax capital inflows, it would be levied by financial institutions on a withholding basis on all receipts of foreign exchange. It could then be refunded on exports through the value added tax (VAT) system and on receipts of income through the income tax system. Any country having both VAT and income tax should therefore have an evasion-resistant way of collecting the tax and rebating it where no tax is due.

The fourth possible form of capital control merits more extended discussion. It has been suggested that a country should create a special foreign exchange market where pension funds, both domestic and foreign, would be required to trade.[5] A first issue is the administrative feasibility

---

4. However, such a tax needs to be very different from a Tobin tax. It needs to be at a much higher rate than the few basis points that most advocates of the Tobin tax now advocate (at least, those who recognize that anything more would provoke a switch to a broker market from the present dealer structure of the foreign exchange market). And it needs to be asymmetrical, that is, imposed only on those who purchase the currency whose value one is trying to keep down.

5. An alternative technique for achieving the same objective would be to limit domestic pension funds to portfolio swaps with foreign pension funds. A variant on that proposal would be for domestic and foreign pension funds to agree to swap the income streams accruing from an index portfolio of the same initial value in each other's markets (first suggested by Lessard 1972). That would achieve the benefits of portfolio diversification and avoid the legal complications of holding shares in another country. However, neither of these variants would permit all the benefits of the approach discussed in the text.

of this proposal. It is one thing to regulate one's own pension funds, but, if the regime applied only to pension funds, foreign pension funds would presumably invest indirectly, via mutual funds, whenever the special rate stood at a premium. Hence, it would be necessary to include mutual funds along with pension funds as being required to invest through any such special market. But that does not appear a priori infeasible: Financial institutions would hardly be tempted to go underground to get a better exchange rate, especially given that they would have to place assets within legal reach of the authorities from whom they were trying to hide.

As it stands, the proposal would preclude a country benefiting from a resource transfer financed by net purchases of portfolio equity on the part of foreign pension (and mutual) funds. Capital inflows from foreign pension funds and mutual funds could be no larger than the capital outflows that domestic pension funds and mutual funds would be able and willing to finance. Even if one accepts the logical case for small countries to encourage their pension funds to invest heavily in foreign securities,[6] on the ground that this would reduce the vulnerability of the nation in general and its retirees in particular to country-specific shocks, one would expect net inflows (at the market exchange rate) for the next decade or two. This is because pension and mutual funds are already close to maturity in most developed countries and therefore hold large stocks of assets, a part of which will be redeployed to emerging markets as these grow in size and become more integrated into the global capital market. In contrast, pension funds in most developing countries are still at a very early stage of development, so that even if they invest a large proportion of their assets abroad this would not match the inflows that could be expected. A large premium on the local currency in the special pension–mutual fund market would therefore be needed to choke off the excess demand for inward investment at the market exchange rate.

But why should a country make a point of principle of insisting that this rate float freely? Why shouldn't the authorities be allowed to intervene in this market, notably by supplying domestic currency and buying foreign exchange when there is an excess demand for inward investment at the market exchange rate? One possible reason is that the country may be suffering a capital surge and trying to limit capital inflows. In that event, allowing a premium in a separate market for pension and mutual funds could be a useful instrument in limiting the excessive capital inflow. Conversely, when there is a large attempt to withdraw funds, for example, because of a speculative crisis, it would make a lot of sense to allow the rate in this special market to go to a discount so as to throttle off the incipient capital outflow. Where the authorities do not confront either dilemma, however, it would seem both possible and sensible for them to intervene

---

6. See Laurence Kotlikoff and Charles Seeger, "Look Abroad to Solve the Pension Crisis," *Financial Times,* April 25, 2000.

to keep the special rate close to the normal market rate. That would in turn limit the rewards from successful evasion and prevent market practitioners from learning how to evade, so that one could hope that the system would be in less danger of being undermined by the growth of evasion.

A potential difficulty in implementing this proposal is that it would amount to a multiple currency practice, which is one of the worst sins in the IMF's lexicon; such practices are specifically prohibited by the Fund's Articles of Agreement. It is silly, however, to treat such a prohibition as inviolable: One should ask whether such practices ought to remain proscribed. It is perfectly sensible to prohibit multiple exchange rates that discriminate among current transactions, for that is a way that governments find it all too easy to give special privileges to elite interests at the expense of the general interest. But the Fund should turn a blind eye if some countries choose to experiment with using a separate market for pension and mutual funds. If and when this is demonstrated to be a feasible and useful technique, the international community should be prepared to amend the Fund's articles to legalize the more general use of the technique.

Would a parallel market for pension and mutual funds be to the disadvantage of Northern investors? Patient holders would still be able to expect to buy and sell most of the time at a rate close to the regular exchange rate. During a panic, the special rate would go to a discount that would still enable them to pick up shares being dumped by panicked investors at bargain rates, so there is no reason why patient investors need suffer. Herd investors would doubtless object and blame their losses on the discount in the parallel rate, and they indeed might be worse off to the extent that the concentration of selling in a narrower market would result in a less favorable rate for them. This then is a change that would discriminate between groups of Northern investors, to the advantage of the ones that emerging markets would benefit by encouraging.

The third issue that was posed above is whether there might still be a role for administrative controls in emergency situations. It is not clear that the Malaysian capital controls imposed in September 1998 did a great deal of good, but they certainly did not have the disastrous effect that many operators in the financial markets initially prophesied; the main criticism that now seems pertinent is that they were not imposed soon enough. Had all the East Asian countries imposed such capital outflow controls early in the crisis in 1997, the effects of the crisis probably would not have been anywhere near as severe as they were. Investors who are terrified of being temporarily locked in by such controls are not the patient investors that capital-importing countries need. Hence, I conclude that the international rules should not proscribe such controls and debtor countries should be prepared to impose such controls if the circumstances ever again demand it. In some cases it might be sensible for a group of countries to impose controls simultaneously, otherwise action by one country would run the risk of imposing contagion on other, similarly situated, countries.

The fourth question is whether the effectiveness of controls tends to erode over time. Although I am not sure that systematic evidence of this exists, it is widely believed to be the case. There is an obvious reason why this belief persists: the process of discovery of loopholes by agents. Certainly it is generally believed in Chile that but for the amendments that were periodically introduced the effectiveness of the URR would have decayed greatly over the half decade it was in use. I conclude that those who plan to use capital controls need to recognize the likelihood that without repeated amendments the effectiveness of the controls is likely to erode over time. Controls should be temporary or, if permanent, they should not normally be costly to the affected party (the parallel market discussed above would not be).

The final issue is how capital account controls should be liberalized in a country that starts off with comprehensive controls in place. Subject to the caveat that the controls are being effectively policed, experience seems to suggest that a process of gradual liberalization is preferable to one of rapid opening. Inflows should be liberalized before outflows, but only after macroeconomic stability has been achieved, trade and the financial system have been liberalized, and the banking system is indubitably solvent. FDI should be liberalized first, followed by trade credit, portfolio equity, and long-term bonds and loans. Because no great welfare gains can be anticipated from liberalizing short-term flows, this should not be a priority. On the other hand, retaining in place a web of controls that has ceased to be effective or necessary is pointless, and one would expect that sooner or later a country would choose to complete its integration into the international capital market.

Currency of Denomination

It was argued in chapter 6 that one factor that has in the past made foreign exchange crises so painful to many emerging markets is that much of their debt was denominated in foreign currencies, as a result of which the burden of servicing debt exploded just when countries were least able to afford it. Chapter 6 discussed two actions that creditors could take in order to ameliorate this problem: The IMF could start reporting currency mismatches, and, more radically, the creditor countries could require their banks to make loans denominated in the currency of the borrower. It was also stated that there is a much longer list of things the borrower countries could do in order to eliminate currency mismatches, and it is to these that we now turn.

Goldstein and Turner (2004) suggest a series of actions, although none is particularly radical. First they urge banks in emerging economies to step up the monitoring of currency mismatches incurred by their borrowers and to apply tighter credit limits on foreign currency loans to customers who do not generate foreign currency revenues. There is always a question of why the banks that make the relevant decisions should take any notice of such advice, so Goldstein and Turner also recommend that bank supervisors strengthen the prudential oversight of currency mismatching by banks themselves and ensure that the latter monitor the currency exposure of their clients. Reportedly it is remarkably effective just to force banks' boards of directors (not simply compliance officers) to sign a statement to supervisors that they have verified that all large foreign currency exposures to corporate clients (other than pure trade finance) do not entail dangerous mismatches for their clients.

Goldstein and Turner also urge supervisors to insist on prompt corrective action and least-cost resolution when banks show the first signs of getting into trouble. They urge that governments pay attention to the composition of their own debt, aiming to reduce the proportion of debt that is denominated in or indexed to a foreign currency if that proportion is initially high. They suggest that inflation-indexed bonds might provide a useful transition device to facilitate that objective. They also urge governments with low foreign exchange reserves relative to repayments and interest due over the following year to aim at higher reserve holdings. And they urge the removal of outdated accounting rules that bias decisions toward foreign currency denominated borrowing.

All these recommendations appear meritorious, although one might wonder why inflation-indexed bonds should be only a transition device rather than (as in the United States) a permanent part of the scenery. But one may still wonder whether some more muscular action is called for. One possibility would be to use the tax system to encourage indebtedness in the national currency rather than some foreign currency. It is not evident why it should be impossible to charge a higher tax rate on the income from assets that are denominated in a foreign currency, or to allow less tax relief on interest that is paid on liabilities that are denominated in foreign currency, or both. Taxpayers would simply have to declare on their tax return the currency of denomination of their assets or liabilities (as those receiving foreign income already declare on their form 1116 in the United States).

This would not resolve the problem of those who hold dollar-denominated assets in some tax haven like Miami, who will continue to pay taxes entirely voluntarily (i.e., extremely rarely) until some appropriate international agreement (withholding or tax information sharing) is concluded between tax havens and emerging markets. Indeed, if the tax incentive were provided by raising the tax on foreign currency denominated assets rather than by cutting the tax on domestic currency denominated assets, it would raise the incentive to cheat by placing one's assets in "Miami." Conceivably this will provide a serious argument in some countries against using a higher tax rate on interest received, but that still would not preclude providing an incentive to avoid mismatching by reducing interest relief on foreign currency liabilities.

An even stronger action on the part of the borrowing countries would be to make foreign currency denominated loans illegal. Anne Krueger (2000, 40) proposed in her pre-IMF days that borrowing countries could make "foreign-currency obligations incurred by domestic entities . . . within their boundaries unenforceable in domestic courts." She argued that because many foreign lenders would still wish to have their receipts secured in terms of a foreign currency, this would "generate the build-up of an offshore forward foreign-exchange market" in which foreign lenders would be able to cover their borrower-country assets. The cost of a currency mismatch would not necessarily be eliminated if the worst materialized, however, because if cover were provided by another domestic entity it would simply transfer the risk within the domestic economy (though presumably to an exporter or some other entity better able to bear it). The cost would be eliminated only if the counterparty were a foreigner. Perhaps an even more serious weakness of the proposal is that emerging-market issuers would still be able to raise loans in foreign markets denominated in foreign currencies provided these were subject to foreign law. For these reasons I prefer the proposal to use the tax system, as outlined above, to discourage mismatching.

GDP-Indexed Bonds

Another very interesting proposal has recently attracted discussion, in part because a variant is playing a role in the Argentinean debt reconstruction and in part because of a revival of interest in the use of contingent financial contracts to enhance macroeconomic stability (Athanasoulis, Shiller, and van Wincoop 1999). This is the issuance of GDP-indexed bonds (Borensztein and Mauro 2004; Council of Economic Advisers 2004).[7] The specific form of the Borensztein-Mauro proposal would involve a bond that promised to pay an interest coupon that depended on the issuing country's rate of growth. In the simplest possible example, a country with a trend rate of growth of 3 percent per year and an ability to borrow on plain-vanilla terms at 7 percent per year might issue bonds with a yield that was 1 percent above or below 7 percent (plus an insurance premium that one would expect to be small[8]) for every 1 percent that its growth rate exceeded or fell short of 3 percent. An alternative would be to specify the interest coupon as a certain percentage of GDP; if that were interpreted as nominal GDP, the formula would achieve a measure of indexation to the

7. Both the Cuzco proposals of the Rio Group of Latin American countries and the 2004 declaration of the Summit of the Americas have expressed support for the idea.

8. Borensztein and Mauro argue that this would be small because investors would have the possibility of diversifying their holding across countries.

price level as well as to real long-run growth. Various other possible formulas are also presented by Borensztein and Mauro (2004, 175, box 1).

This proposal has two big advantages from the standpoint of an emerging-market borrower. One is that it would provide significant relief when growth was unusually low in return for a requirement of higher payments at times when the country was in a position to pay more. The other advantage is that it would limit cyclical fiscal pressures because it would require the payment of larger sums at times the budget was strong owing to prosperity and rapid growth while it would limit the deterioration of the budget in bad times when growth was weak. The Borensztein-Mauro proposal would thus go some way toward curbing the pressures that have in the past been responsible for most emerging markets running procyclical fiscal policies. Because an economy that grows persistently more slowly than expected would experience lower interest obligations, its ratio of debt to GDP would tend to increase more slowly; it would thus be less likely to end up in a financial crisis.

From the standpoint of the lender, the big issue is whether it could have confidence that the terms of the contract would be honored. Borrowing countries would have an incentive to underreport (but certainly not to reduce!) their growth rates, so as to reduce their interest obligations. This might argue for making the statistical agency formally independent of government, like many central banks are nowadays. Also, it would surely require having some international agency, perhaps the IMF, monitor and verify the figures reported by the borrower. The question is whether the lender would find this adequate to instill confidence that the figures were not being misreported so as to reduce financial obligations. On the plus side, one can note that national income accounting is by now a fairly standard procedure and, also, that on every other ground a government usually has an incentive to overreport rather than to underreport growth. One still has to acknowledge that there is inevitably some element of subjective judgment in estimating the growth rate, and some investors are likely to fear that this could be abused in some emerging markets. The issue is not whether growth rates will be accurate, for elements of subjectivity and uncertainty are inevitable, but whether the fear of willful doctoring of the figures can be laid to rest.

Skeptics question whether GDP-indexed bonds could be expected to trade in liquid markets because of the data and computational problems that arise in computing their value. This is surely based on a misconception, for the valuation of equities is even less well defined by objective circumstances. What matters is that a well-defined authority in which investors have confidence is responsible for determining the sum that will be paid out in a given situation. One can have doubts as to whether investors would have confidence in a purely national authority (given that investors would not have the fallback right of approving a takeover that presumably assures them that the managers of a company will more or less stay in line with shareholder interests), but such doubt says that the international community should ask itself whether it can help instill the necessary confidence. Neither traders in the market nor investors need concern themselves with the problems of data and computation, except insofar as they help them forecast.

One should also note that, from the standpoint of the lender, GDP-indexed bonds have two potentially important attractions. One (which as already noted is also an attraction for the debtor) is that they would be less likely to lead a country into financial crisis, with the subsequent possibility of a costly debt reconstruction. The other is that some investors will welcome the opportunity such bonds offer of taking a position on the future growth prospects of particular countries.[9] As the Council of Economic Advisers (2004) noted in its white paper on the subject, growth-indexed bonds would allow countries to adopt a liability structure (with an equity component) that is popular for companies but not previously available for sovereigns.

A variant of the proposal for a GDP-indexed bond would also offer the advantage of providing de facto local currency denomination. This variant would have the bonds offering a coupon payment of a certain (minute) percentage of the country's measured GDP, with GDP calculated at the market exchange rate rather than at purchasing power parity. An exchange rate appreciation, which often occurs during a boom, would then result in higher payments—just at the time when the country is in a position to afford them and, indeed, when they may play a helpful role in increasing payment obligations and thus limiting the exchange rate appreciation. When a country encounters problems, its currency is likely to depreciate, thus reducing its coupon payments and limiting the strain on both budget and balance of payments position.

A Program

Just as at the end of the previous chapter we compiled a list of the set of actions on the part of creditors that the analysis had suggested could contribute to smoothing the boom-bust cycle, so it is appropriate to conclude this chapter by making a similar list of actions by the debtors that would help mitigate boom and bust.

This chapter started by reviewing the conditions for a responsible macroeconomic policy that are an indispensable prerequisite for curbing any sort of cycle. These are crucial because many of the proposals in this program could be abused in order to allow countries to go further into

---

9. If this attraction were sufficiently important, it is in principle conceivable that a GDP-indexed bond could be sold with a discount from the plain-vanilla interest rate instead of at the premium that is normally assumed.

debt. If the proposals are to benefit the countries that adopt them, it is necessary that they not simply be used to provide more rope with which countries can hang themselves. It was then acknowledged that improved bank supervision—particularly by the introduction of forward-looking provisioning—and the development of local bond markets could play a key role in damping down volatility.

The chapter then turned to the issue of capital controls. No one wishes to see old-fashioned prohibitions and restrictions that require the use of administrative discretion, but neither does it seem sensible to expose emerging markets to the full force of the gales that come from changing market sentiment. Of the various ways of limiting exposure to capital flows, four were suggested as potentially useful (bearing in mind the importance of recommending only what is administratively practical). One is temporary use of the traditional approach (prohibitions and administratively enforced restrictions) to curb or prevent capital outflows (or borrowing by foreigners) at times of crisis. A second is the use of a URR to discourage inflows when these are threatening to be excessive. A third is the taxation of capital flows, which would be very similar to a URR (except that it could also apply to portfolio equity) if applied to inflows but could also be applied to outflows. The fourth is the creation of a parallel foreign exchange market, where pension funds and mutual funds would be obliged to transact.

Such a program (and also an international environment that looked charitably on the continued maintenance of other forms of capital controls) would depend on endorsement by the main developed countries in the IMF and their agreement to change the IMF articles to abandon the proscription on dual foreign exchange markets. In addition, it would require that the United States terminate its current policy of using bilateral free trade agreements as instruments to bully small countries into emasculating all efforts to use capital controls to protect themselves against the vicissitudes of the ebb and flow of capital.

The chapter endorsed the view that borrowing in a currency other than the country's own makes a country vulnerable to crisis and should, therefore, be largely phased out as rapidly as possible. It also subscribed to the view that emerging markets can do a series of things to change the currency composition of their debt, and it dismissed the alternative view that foreign currency borrowing is inevitable because of original sin. Emerging markets should certainly phase out or, at first, at least cut back public-sector borrowing in foreign currencies. Bank supervisors should insist on the banks themselves maintaining a balanced foreign currency position and curbing lending to nontradable sectors in foreign currencies. Of more radical actions, the chapter noted but did not endorse Anne Krueger's proposal that countries should simply make foreign exchange debts unenforceable in their domestic courts. It was argued that a much better approach would be to give a fiscal incentive for use of the local currency in denominating debt contracts by charging a higher tax rate on interest paid on loans denominated in foreign currency, by allowing less tax relief on such interest, or both.

The chapter concluded by endorsing the proposal to have emerging markets issue GDP-linked bonds. Such bonds would vary a country's interest obligations in accordance with its ability to pay. This would have the advantages of making it less likely that a country would find itself unable to pay its contractual interest obligations in bad circumstances and would also build in an element of countercyclical fiscal policy, inasmuch as expenditures on debt service would automatically increase in good times.

8

An Action Program

It has been taken for granted throughout this study that the major flows of capital from developed countries to emerging markets will be organized through the private sector. That is not to dismiss the role of the public sector, which will remain of critical importance in the poorest and least creditworthy countries, in responding to financial and humanitarian emergencies, and in the provision of international public goods. It is now abundantly clear, however, that countries that have advanced to the point where they are capable of absorbing significant sums will in the future look mainly to the private markets.

The historical experience with private capital flows has been punctuated by crises that were costly for both creditors and borrowers. Recent years have witnessed much discussion of how these can be avoided in the future. In addition to the customary exhortations to emerging markets to run responsible policies regarding macroeconomic management and bank supervision and to press forward with the development of local bond markets and the implementation of standards and codes, this study endorsed a number of proposals that collectively constitute an action program.

1. Adoption of forward-looking provisioning on the Spanish model by commercial banks in all countries, so that it would cover both loans to emerging markets from banks in industrial countries and the operations of banks in emerging markets.

2. Calculation of the reported maturity of bonds by the time until the next put option falls due instead of by the time until the bond matures if put options are never exercised.

3. Adoption of the prudent-man principle to govern the investment decisions of insurance companies to replace regulations that limit insurance companies to holding investment-grade bonds. If this suggestion is too radical, the minimum that should be done is replace the requirement that insurance companies *hold* only investment-grade bonds with an amended requirement that says they may *acquire* only investment-grade bonds.

4. Retention of the right and ability of emerging markets to use capital controls in certain situations. Even prohibitions and administrative restrictions should be allowed if necessary in times of crisis. Normally such measures should be avoided, and any needed influence over capital flows should be achieved via (1) the imposition of uncompensated reserve requirements (on the Chilean model), (2) the taxation of capital flows, or (3) the creation of a parallel foreign exchange market through which pension funds and mutual funds would be obliged to channel their transactions.

5. Creation of a fiscal incentive for borrowers and lenders in emerging markets to issue and hold assets denominated in local currency.

6. A switch in the lending policies of the MDBs on the lines advocated by Eichengreen and Hausmann (2003). MDBs would borrow in a new synthetic currency unit, the value of which would be defined by a basket of emerging-market currencies indexed to the countries' CPIs. The MDBs would largely avoid currency exposure by lending to emerging markets in their own currencies, on an indexed basis, in roughly the same proportions that the basket is composed. This would eliminate currency mismatches in the borrowing of emerging markets from MDBs without exposing the MDBs to significant currency risk.

7. Limitation (and maybe ultimate elimination) of foreign currency borrowing by emerging-market governments. Instead, these governments should start issuing GDP-linked bonds on the international market and inflation-indexed bonds and plain-vanilla bonds denominated in the national currency on their local markets.

These recommendations may be divided into three categories. Some are suggestions for ways of doing things differently from how they are done at the moment, but they essentially suggest alternative rules for things that have to be done in any event. In this category one might place the first three recommendations on the preceding list. For example, banks are going to be subject to rules that govern how many provisions they have to put aside against bad loans; the first recommendation is that the rules should require them to look forward and estimate how much they will ultimately need to put aside if statistical experience is normal rather than wait for bad events to materialize. Similarly, rules exist that govern the reported maturity of bonds, and the issue dealt with in the second recommendation is whether the maturity that has to be reported should represent a period over which the borrower can rely on not having to repay. Again, insurance companies are subject to regulations; the question is what the substance of those regulations should be.

A second set of recommendations deals with yes-no questions. A country may decide to forgo capital controls and operate with a completely open capital account, or it may decide to retain capital controls. The fourth recommendation above argues that, if an emerging-market country is serious about controlling the boom-bust cycle, it needs to retain the possibility of resorting to capital controls in certain situations. For emerging markets to be able to resort to capital controls when necessary, the country itself must be convinced that this is appropriate, but the developed countries also need to be supportive. They will have to stop inserting clauses in bilateral free trade agreements that could emasculate the use of capital controls by their trading partners, and they may need to support a revision of the IMF's Articles of Agreement that will withdraw the blanket proscription of multiple exchange rates that is presently embodied in the Articles. The fifth recommendation is that countries should create a fiscal incentive to encourage their residents to use the national currency rather than a foreign currency for denominating debt contracts. It is perfectly possible to envisage a world without such an incentive—indeed, that is the world we are living in. Or it is possible to envisage a world with only a limited pressure to diminish foreign currency mismatches, for this is what Goldstein and Turner (2004) propose. The text argues that one should go further and use a fiscal incentive.

Recommendations in the third category are perhaps the most radical. They involve the creation of new financial instruments—bonds whose value is determined by an indexed basket of emerging-market currencies in the sixth case, and GDP-indexed bonds in the last case. Not all economists (for example, Rajan 2004) are in favor of "clever solutions," as they have been dismissively termed. These economists argue that, if the market has not already come up with such an instrument, this is probably because there is something wrong with it. That is possible, and any such proposal should indeed be examined carefully. However, many innovations have eventually been accepted by the financial markets (compare the multiplicity of instruments that are available nowadays with what the markets used to offer, say, 30 years ago). In some cases, ideas were suggested and lay around unexploited for many years, until one day their use exploded. Collective action clauses in sovereign bond contracts, to cite a recent example, were first advocated by Eichengreen and Portes in 1995, but they were adopted in the standard New York bond issued by emerging markets only in 2003. Or "the market for credit default swaps remained small for years but took off rapidly as soon as the standards for a 'credit event' were properly defined and became broadly accepted" (Borensztein and Mauro 2004, 189).

One clearly needs to ask why financial innovation that could be of general benefit might fail to occur. This subject is explored in some depth by Borensztein and Mauro (2004) in the paper in which they develop the case for GDP-indexed bonds. They suggest five possible impediments to beneficial financial innovation:[1]

- **Critical mass.** New and complex instruments may be illiquid. Pricing them involves computational costs. Launching a new instrument therefore requires a concerted effort to achieve critical mass so as to attain market liquidity and spread computational costs. For example, in the particular case of GDP-indexed bonds, the reduction in default risk that is one of the major expected benefits will be realized only once the share of the debt held in these bonds is substantial.

- **Product uncertainty.** Investors are uncertain about the nature of a new financial instrument and will therefore hold it only if offered a premium, but such a premium may deter borrowers from issuing the new instrument. No individual borrower will wish to bear the costs of pioneering a new instrument. There is an infant-market benefit of such pioneering that may merit some form of social subsidy.

- **Externalities and coordination problems.** A large number of borrowers have to issue a new financial instrument before investors can diversify risk by holding an appropriate portfolio of similar instruments. However, an individual borrower will not take into account the social benefit of assisting others issue similar instruments. The holders of GDP-indexed bonds are not rewarded for reducing the likelihood that the borrowing country will be forced to default and impose losses on the holders of plain-vanilla bonds.

- **Competition in financial markets.** A private financial institution that develops a new financial instrument will incur costs that it will be unable to recoup by maintaining a subsequent monopoly over its provision because such instruments are in general not patentable and imitation of a successful innovation is easy. The private incentive to develop such instruments is therefore low even if the social benefit is high.

- **Need for standardization.** A liquid secondary market where investors are able to diversify their portfolios requires instruments with the same features for all the issuers. This is particularly important for con-

---

1. They acknowledge that their list was inspired by Allen and Gale (1994).

ditional instruments where the size of the payment depends on certain standards that need to be unambiguous, verifiable, and similar.

These considerations provide ample grounds for understanding why the fact that a financial innovation is socially desirable does not necessarily lead to its adoption by the markets. Indeed, the preceding list offers a compelling explanation of why the markets so often appear to some of us to be absurdly conservative. But the international community has certain organizations—specifically, the international financial institutions—that it can potentially use to further internationally desired objectives, such as socially beneficial innovations in international financial instruments. One should therefore ask whether there are reasons for believing that the two innovations advocated in this study—MDB bonds denominated in a basket of indexed emerging-market currencies and GDP-linked bonds—could be fostered by the international financial institutions.

Consider first the Eichengreen-Hausmann proposal for the World Bank to issue bonds denominated in a basket of indexed emerging-market currencies. This proposal is, in fact, one for the World Bank itself. Admittedly the World Bank's treasury department would have to take an initiative of a character that it has not in the past been keen to grasp, but if the international community—presumably in the form of the International Monetary and Financial Committee—instructed the Bank that it wanted this done, the Bank's treasury department would possess all the needed technical skills.

The only possible reason I can see to question whether this proposal could be successfully initiated by the World Bank is that some economists (e.g., my colleagues Goldstein and Turner 2004) doubt whether investors could be persuaded to buy bonds denominated in a unit with which they are not familiar. They talk about how complicated a basket of indexed emerging-market currencies would be, even though it is far less complex than many of the derivatives nowadays traded in financial markets. Eichengreen and Hausmann have shown that on past experience such a basket would be no more variable in terms of the dollar than the currencies of other industrial countries in which it is perfectly possible to issue bonds. Hence, I see little reason to doubt that, given a premium, investors could be persuaded to buy and hold such assets. As familiarity grew, they might even cease to demand a premium (especially since the inflation-proofing feature implies that this bond would tend to appreciate over time in terms of the currencies of most or all industrial countries).

In contrast, GDP-linked bonds would be issued by the governments of emerging-market countries rather than by an international organization, so that they could not be launched directly by an international initiative as in the previous case. Unfortunately, the obstacles to a decentralized initiative that were discussed above are sufficiently acute to make spontaneous action by an individual country unlikely, at least outside of a debt-restructuring exercise. Perhaps the use of bonds with a GDP growth link in order to give investors an upside bonus, as in the Argentinean debt restructuring, is the way that such bonds will be introduced into investors' portfolios in the short run although it is not clear that the link with Argentina will impress investors with the desirability of this innovation. Even if GDP-linked bonds gain a toehold in this way, some form of initiative by an international organization like the IMF or World Bank might be able to help generalize a market in GDP-linked bonds. This issue too is considered by Borensztein and Mauro (2004, 204).

> Possible areas where international financial institutions could play a role in fostering the creation of a market for GDP-indexed bonds include promoting their use through the dialogue with member countries and encouraging country authorities to take a longer horizon perspective than is often dictated by electoral cycles; gauging interest for these securities among potential investors, and providing information on the likelihood that a critical mass of issuing countries would be willing to use GDP-indexed bonds; encouraging countries to ensure the independence of their statistical agencies and providing technical assistance to improve the quality and transparency of national income statistics, and helping guarantee their reliability; and gathering the necessary information for pricing the instruments, including estimates of co-movement of output among countries and the relationship between economic variables and default risk.

My own guess is that a formal role for some international organization, probably the IMF, in guaranteeing the reliability of national income statistics would be an essential condition for such a market to function. Beyond that, an initiative for a joint swap of a substantial part of emerging-market debt into GDP-linked bonds would probably best come from a group of emerging markets themselves, with an organization like the IMF responding to a request from them to undertake the nitty-gritty of coordination. This seems the best hope for establishing GDP-linked bonds as a regular and important vehicle for the foreign sovereign borrowing of emerging markets.

Can one prioritize among the seven items in the action program suggested at the beginning of this chapter? No one could claim that the suggested reforms, from reporting bond maturities as the time remaining to the next put option to the introduction of GDP-linked bonds, are of equal importance. Prioritization makes sense only if the reforms are in some way competitive with one another, and they are certainly not competitive in the sense that adopting any one of them would preclude any of the others. If they are competitive at all, it can only be because reformers have a limited amount of time and energy and can therefore be expected to focus on only one or two reforms at a time. If that is a real constraint, the most demanding reforms would seem to be those that call for the introduction of new financial instruments (reforms 6 and 7), while perhaps the biggest bang for the buck would be offered by reforms 1 and 4 (forward-looking provisioning and retention of the right to impose capital controls). Prioritization would make no sense at all if it were true that all the reforms must be implemented as a package deal in order to make any impact on the boom-bust cycle, but this too seems untenable. Rather, this is a case where any reforms should be welcomed and the more the merrier.

The boom-bust cycle in capital flows has driven the cycle of the emerging markets for the past three decades. Some cyclical fluctuations seem to be an inherent feature of the financial markets of capitalist economies, but their relatively benign form in the industrial countries in the 60 years since World War II demonstrates that they do not have to be as destructive as they have been in the emerging markets. The action program that has been developed in this study is intended to facilitate a process of financial maturing similar to the one that has already occurred in the industrial countries.

References

Alesina, Alberto, Vittorio Grilli, and Gian Maria Milesi-Ferretti. 1994. The Political Economy of Capital Controls. In *Capital Mobility: The Impact on Consumption and Growth*, ed. L. Leiderman and A. Razin. Cambridge, England: Cambridge University Press.

Allen, F., and D. Gale. 1994. *Financial Innovation and Risk Sharing*. Cambridge, MA: MIT Press.

Artana, Daniel, Ricardo López Murphy, and Fernando Navajas. 2003. A Fiscal Policy Agenda. In *After the Washington Consensus: Restarting Growth and Reform in Latin America*, ed. Pedro-Pablo Kuczynski and John Williamson. Washington: Institute for International Economics.

Athanasoulis, Stefano, Robert Shiller, and Eric van Wincoop. 1999. Macro Markets and Financial Stability. *Federal Reserve Bank of New York Economic Policy Review* 5, no. 1 (April): 21–39.

Barth, Michael, and Xin Zhang. 1999. Foreign Equity Flows and the Asian Financial Crisis. In *The Crisis in Emerging Financial Markets*, World Bank–Brookings Institution Conference on Finance and Development, March 26–27. Washington: World Bank and Brookings Institution Press.

Bekaert, Geert, Campbell R. Harvey, and Robin L. Lumsdaine. 1999. *The Dynamics of Emerging Market Equity Flows*. NBER Working Paper 7219. Cambridge, MA: National Bureau of Economic Research.

Bekaert, Geert, Campbell R. Harvey, and Christina Lundblad. 2001. *Does Financial Liberalization Spur Growth?* NBER Working Paper 8245. Cambridge, MA: National Bureau of Economic Research.

Berg, Andrew. 1999. *The Asia Crisis: Causes, Policy Responses, and Outcomes*. IMF Working Paper 99/138. Washington: International Monetary Fund.

Bernard, Henri, and Joseph Bisagnano. 1999. Information, Liquidity and Risk in the International Interbank Market: Implicit Guarantees and Private Credit Market Failure. Bank for International Settlements, Basel. Photocopy.

Berthelemy, Jean-Claude, and Sophie Chauvin. 2000. *Structural Changes in Asia and Growth Prospects after the Crisis*. Paris: Centre d'Études Prospectives et d'Informations Internationales.

Bevan, David L., Paul Collier, and Jan Willem Gunning. 1999. *The Political Economy of Poverty, Equity, and Growth: Nigeria and Indonesia*. New York: Oxford University Press for the World Bank.

Bordo, Michael D. 1999. An Historical Perspective on Financial Crisis Policy. Paper prepared for the annual meetings of the American Economic Association, January.

Bordo, Michael, Barry Eichengreen, Daniela Klingebiel, and M. Soledad Martinez-Peria. 2001. Is the Crisis Problem Growing More Severe? *Economic Policy* (April): 1–51.

Borensztein, Eduardo, and Paolo Mauro. 2004. The Case for GDP-Indexed Bonds. *Economic Policy* (April): 165–216.

Brecher, Richard A., and Carlos Diaz-Alejandro. 1977. Tariffs, Foreign Capital, and Immiserizing Growth. *Journal of International Economics 7*, no. 4 (November): 353–60.

Broner, Fernando A., Guido Lorenzoni, and Sergio L. Schmukler. 2004. Why Do Emerging Economies Borrow Short Term? World Bank Policy Research Paper 3389 (August). Washington: World Bank.

Bryant, Ralph C. 2003. *Turbulent Waters: Cross-Border Finance and International Governance.* Washington: Brookings Institution Press.

Buchheit, Lee C., and G. Mitu Gulati. 2000. Exit Consents in Sovereign Bond Exchanges. *UCLA Law Review 48*, no. 1 (October): 59–84.

Buiter, Willem H., and Anne C. Sibert. 1999. UDROP: A Contribution to the New International Financial Architecture. *International Finance 2*, no. 2 (July): 227–48.

Calvo, Guillermo, Leonardo Leiderman, and Carmen Reinhart. 1993. Capital Inflows and Real Exchange Rate Appreciation in Latin America: The Role of External Factors. *IMF Staff Papers 40*, no. 1 (March): 108–51.

Choe, Hyuk, Bong-Chan Kho, and Rene M. Stulz. 1998. *Do Foreign Investors Destabilize Stock Markets? The Korean Experience in 1997.* NBER Working Paper 6661. Cambridge, MA: National Bureau of Economic Research.

Claessens, Stijn, Michael Dooley, and Andrew Warner. 1994. Portfolio Capital Flows: Hot or Cool? In *Investing in Emerging Markets,* ed. M. J. Howell. London: Euromoney Publications in association with the World Bank.

Collier, Paul. 2000. Consensus-Building, Knowledge, and Conditionality. Paper presented at annual World Bank conference on development economics, Washington.

Committee for Economic Development. 2000. *Improving Global Financial Stability: A Policy Statement by the Research and Policy Committee of the Committee for Economic Development.* New York: Committee for Economic Development.

Committee on the Global Financial System. 2004. *Foreign Direct Investment in the Financial Sector of Emerging Market Economies.* Basel: Bank for International Settlements.

Cooper, Richard N. 1999. Should Capital Controls Be Banished? *Brookings Papers on Economic Activity* 1. Washington: Brookings Institution Press.

Corden, W. Max. 2002. *Too Sensational: On the Choice of Exchange Rate Regimes.* Cambridge, MA: MIT Press.

Council of Economic Advisers. 2004. *Growth-Indexed Bonds: A Primer.* Washington: Council of Economic Advisers.

Diwan, Ishac. 1999. Labor Shares and Financial Crises. Paper presented at conference of the Global Development Network, December, Bonn.

Dobson, Wendy, and Gary Hufbauer. 2001. *World Capital Markets: Challenge to the G-10.* Washington: Institute for International Economics.

Dooley, Michael P., David Folkerts-Landau, and Peter Garber. 2003. *An Essay on the Revived Bretton Woods System.* NBER Working Paper 9971. Cambridge, MA: National Bureau of Economic Research.

Edison, Hali J., Ross Levine, Luca Ricci, and Torsten Sløk. 2002. International Financial Integration and Economic Growth. *Journal of International Money and Finance 21*, no. 6 (November): 749–76.

Eichengreen, Barry, and Ricardo Hausmann. 2003. The Road to Redemption. In *Other People's Money: Debt Denomination and Financial Instability in Emerging-Market Economies,* ed. B. Eichengreen and R. Hausmann. Chicago: University of Chicago Press.

Eichengreen, Barry, and Peter H. Lindert, eds. 1989. *The International Debt Crisis in Historical Perspective.* Cambridge, MA: MIT Press.

Eichengreen, Barry, and Ashoka Mody. 2000a. *Would Collective Action Clauses Raise Borrowing Costs?* NBER Working Paper 7458. Cambridge, MA: National Bureau of Economic Research.

Eichengreen, Barry, and Ashoka Mody. 2000b. *Would Collective Action Clauses Raise Borrowing Costs? An Update and Extension.* World Bank Working Paper 2363. Washington: World Bank.

Eichengreen, Barry, and Michael Mussa. 1998. *Capital Account Liberalization: Theoretical and Practical Aspects.* Occasional Paper 172. Washington: International Monetary Fund.

Eichengreen, Barry, and Richard Portes. 1995. *Crisis? What Crisis? Orderly Workouts for Sovereign Debtors.* London: Centre for Economic Policy Research.

Ffrench-Davis, Ricardo, and H. Tapia. 2001. Three Policy Varieties to Face Capital Surges in Chile. In *Financial Crises in "Successful" Emerging Economies,* ed. R. Ffrench-Davis. Santiago: McGraw Hill.

Friedman, Thomas L. 1999. *The Lexus and the Olive Tree.* New York: Farrar, Straus, Giroux.

Froot, Kenneth, Paul O'Connell, and Mark Seasholes. 1998. *The Portfolio Flows of International Investors, I.* NBER Working Paper 6687. Cambridge, MA: National Bureau of Economic Research.

Furman, Jason, and Joseph E. Stiglitz. 1998. Economic Crises: Evidence and Insights from East Asia. *Brookings Papers on Economic Activity* 2. Washington: Brookings Institution Press.

Gavin, Michael, Ricardo Hausmann, and Leonardo Leiderman. 1995. *The Macroeconomics of Capital Flows to Latin America: Experience and Policy Issues.* Working Paper 310. Washington: InterAmerican Development Bank.

Goldstein, Morris, and Philip Turner. 2004. *Controlling Currency Mismatches in Emerging Markets.* Washington: Institute for International Economics.

Gourinchas, Pierre-Olivier, and Olivier Jeanne. 2004. *The Elusive Gains from International Financial Integration.* IMF Working Paper 04/74. Washington: International Monetary Fund.

Group of Ten (G-10). 1996. Report of the G-10 Deputies on Sovereign Liquidity Crises.

Henry, Peter Blair. 2000a. Do Stock Market Liberalizations Cause Investment Booms? *Journal of Financial Economics* 58, no. 1–2 (October): 301–34.

Henry, Peter Blair. 2000b. Stock Market Liberalization, Economic Reform, and Emerging Market Equity Prices. *Journal of Finance* 50, no. 2 (April): 529–64.

Hymer, Stephen H. 1960. *The International Operations of National Firms: A Study of Direct Investment.* PhD dissertation, Massachusetts Institute of Technology, Cambridge, MA.

IFIAC (International Financial Institution Advisory Committee). 2000. *Report of the International Financial Institution Advisory Committee.* Washington: No publisher specified.

IMF (International Monetary Fund). 2003. *IMF and Recent Capital Account Crises.* Washington: International Monetary Fund.

Jeanne, Olivier. 2000. *Debt Maturity and the Global Financial Architecture.* CEPR Discussion Paper 2520. London: Centre for Economic Policy Research.

Jeanne, Olivier. 2003. *Why Do Emerging Markets Borrow in Foreign Currency?* IMF Working Paper WP/03/177. Washington: International Monetary Fund.

Kaminsky, Graciela, Richard Lyons, and Sergio Schmukler. 2000. Managers, Investors, and Crises: Mutual Fund Strategy in Emerging Markets. World Bank Working Paper 2399. Washington: World Bank.

Kapur, Devesh, John P. Lewis, and Richard Webb. 1997. *The World Bank: Its First Half Century.* Washington: Brookings Institution Press.

Kaufman, Henry. 2000. *On Money and Markets: A Wall Street Memoir.* New York: McGraw-Hill.

Kim, Woochan, and Shang-Jin Wei. 1999a. *Foreign Portfolio Investors Before and During a Crisis.* NBER Working Paper 6968. Cambridge, MA: National Bureau of Economic Research.

Kim, Woochan, and Shang-Jin Wei. 1999b. *Offshore Investment Funds: Monsters in Emerging Markets?* NBER Working Paper 7133. Cambridge, MA: National Bureau of Economic Research.

Kraay, Aart. 1998. In Search of the Macroeconomic Effects of Capital Account Liberalization. World Bank, Washington. Photocopy.

Krueger, Anne O. 2000. Conflicting Demands on the International Monetary Fund. *American Economic Review* 90, no. 2 (May): 38–42.

Krugman, Paul. 1998. What Happened to Asia? Massachusetts Institute of Technology, Cambridge, MA. Photocopy.

Kupiec, Paul H., and James M. O'Brien. 1997. The Pre-Commitment Approach: Using Incentives to Set Market Risk Capital Requirements. http://smealsearch2.psu.edu/kupiec97 precommitment.html (accessed May 26, 2005).

Lee, Charles M.C., Andrei Shleifer, and Richard H. Thaler. 1990. Anomalies: Closed-End Mutual Funds. *Journal of Economic Perspectives* 4, no. 4 (Fall): 153–64.

Lessard, Donald. 1972. En Pro de Una Union Latinoamericana de Inversiones. *CEMLA Bulletin* (December): 1–14.

Lessard, Donald, and John Williamson. 1985. *Financial Intermediation Beyond the Debt Crisis.* Washington: Institute for International Economics.

Lucas, Robert E. 1990. Why Doesn't Capital Flow from Rich to Poor Countries? *American Economic Review* 80, no. 2 (May): 92–96.

McKinnon, Ronald I., and Hugh Pill. 1999. Exchange-Rate Regimes for Emerging Markets: Moral Hazard and International Overborrowing. *Oxford Review of Economic Policy* 15, no. 3 (Autumn): 19–38.

Moran, Theodore H. 1998. *Foreign Direct Investment and Development.* Washington: Institute for International Economics.

Obstfeld, Maurice. 1994. Risk Taking, Global Diversification, and Growth. *American Economic Review* 84, no. 5 (December): 1310–29.

Ocampo, José Antonio. 2003. Capital Account and Countercyclical Prudential Regulations in Developing Countries. In *From Capital Surges to Drought: Seeking Stability for Emerging Economies,* ed. R. Ffrench-Davis and S. Griffith-Jones. Basingstoke: Palgrave Macmillan for the United Nations University/World Institute for Development Economics Research.

Persaud, Avinash. 2000. Sending the Herd Off the Cliff Edge: The Disturbing Interaction Between Herding and Market-Sensitive Risk Management Practices. Winning essay in the Jacques de Larosière Essay Competition, Institute of International Finance, Washington.

Prasad, Eswar, Kenneth Rogoff, Shang-Jin Wei, and M. Ayhan Kose. 2003. *Effects of Financial Globalization on Some Developing Countries: Some Empirical Evidence.* Washington: International Monetary Fund.

Quinn, Dennis. 1997. The Correlates of Changes in International Financial Regulation. *American Political Science Review* 91, no. 3 (September): 531–51.

Radelet, Steven, and Jeffrey Sachs. 1998. The East Asian Financial Crisis: Diagnosis, Remedies, and Prospects. *Brookings Papers on Economic Activity* 1. Washington: Brookings Institution Press.

Rajan, Raghuram. 2004. How Useful Are Clever Solutions? *Finance and Development* 41, no. 1 (March): 56–57.

Ranciere, Romain, Aaron Tornell, and Frank Westermann. 2005. *Systemic Crises and Growth.* NBER Working Paper 11076. Cambridge, MA: National Bureau of Economic Research.

Reinhart, Carmen M., Kenneth S. Rogoff, and Miguel A. Savastano. 2003. Debt Intolerance. *Brookings Papers on Economic Activity* 1. Washington: Brookings Institution Press.

Rodrik, Dani. 1998. Who Needs Capital Account Convertibility? In *Should the IMF Pursue Capital Account Convertibility?* ed. S. Fischer et al. Essay in International Finance 207. Princeton, NJ: Princeton University.

Rodrik, Dani, and Andrés Velasco. 1999. Short-term Capital Flows. NBER Working Paper 7364. Cambridge, MA: National Bureau of Economic Research.

Rogoff, Kenneth S. 1999. International Institutions for Reducing Global Financial Instability. *Journal of Economic Perspectives* 13, no. 4 (Fall): 21–42.

Swensen, David F. 2000. *Pioneering Portfolio Management: An Unconventional Approach to Institutional Investment.* New York: Free Press.

Talvi, Ernesto, and Carlos A. Vegh. 2000. *Tax Base Variability and Procyclical Fiscal Policy*. NBER Working Paper 7499. Cambridge, MA: National Bureau of Economic Research.

Truman, Edwin M. 2003. *Inflation Targeting in the World Economy*. Washington: Institute for International Economics.

Williamson, John. 1998. Crawling Bands or Monitoring Bands: How to Manage Exchange Rates in a World of Capital Mobility. *International Finance* 1, no. 1 (October): 59–79.

Williamson, John. 2000. *Exchange Rate Regimes for Emerging Markets: Reviving the Intermediate Option*. Washington: Institute for International Economics.

Williamson, John. 2003. Exchange-Rate Policy and Development. Paper presented at a conference sponsored by the Initiative for Policy Dialogue, Barcelona.

Williamson, John. 2004. The Years of Emerging Market Crises. *Journal of Economic Literature* 42, no. 3 (September).

World Bank. 1997. *Private Capital Flows to Developing Countries: The Road to Financial Integration*. New York: Oxford University Press for the World Bank.

World Bank. 1998. *Assessing Aid: What Works, What Doesn't, and Why*. New York: Oxford University Press for the World Bank.

Zee, Howell. 1999. Retarding Short-Term Capital Inflows Through a Withholding Tax. International Monetary Fund, Washington. Photocopy.

Zhang, Liqing. 2004. *Capital Account Liberalization and Financial Instability: A Study Based on the Experience in Emerging Market Economies*. Beijing: Beijing University Press.

Index

Other Publications from the Institute for International Economics

* = out of print

POLICY ANALYSES IN
INTERNATIONAL ECONOMICS Series

1 The Lending Policies of the International
  Monetary Fund*   John Williamson
  August 1982   ISBN 0-88132-000-5
2 "Reciprocity": A New Approach to World
  Trade Policy?*   William R. Cline
  September 1982   ISBN 0-88132-001-3
3 Trade Policy in the 1980s*
  C. Fred Bergsten and William R. Cline
  November 1982   ISBN 0-88132-002-1
4 International Debt and the Stability of the
  World Economy*   William R. Cline
  September 1983   ISBN 0-88132-010-2
5 The Exchange Rate System,* Second Edition
  John Williamson
  Sept. 1983, rev. June 1985   ISBN 0-88132-034-X
6 Economic Sanctions in Support of Foreign
  Policy Goals*
  Gary Clyde Hufbauer and Jeffrey J. Schott
  October 1983   ISBN 0-88132-014-5
7 A New SDR Allocation?*   John Williamson
  March 1984   ISBN 0-88132-028-5
8 An International Standard for Monetary
  Stabilization*   Ronald L. McKinnon
  March 1984   ISBN 0-88132-018-8
9 The Yen/Dollar Agreement: Liberalizing
  Japanese Capital Markets*   Jeffrey A. Frankel
  December 1984   ISBN 0-88132-035-8
10 Bank Lending to Developing Countries: The
   Policy Alternatives*   C. Fred Bergsten,
   William R. Cline, and John Williamson
   April 1985   ISBN 0-88132-032-3
11 Trading for Growth: The Next Round of
   Trade Negotiations*
   Gary Clyde Hufbauer and Jeffrey J. Schott
   September 1985   ISBN 0-88132-033-1
12 Financial Intermediation Beyond the Debt
   Crisis*   Donald R. Lessard, John Williamson
   September 1985   ISBN 0-88132-021-8
13 The United States-Japan Economic Problem*
   C. Fred Bergsten and William R. Cline
   October 1985, 2d ed. January 1987
                             ISBN 0-88132-060-9
14 Deficits and the Dollar: The World Economy
   at Risk*   Stephen Marris
   December 1985, 2d ed. November 1987
                             ISBN 0-88132-067-6
15 Trade Policy for Troubled Industries*
   Gary Clyde Hufbauer and Howard R. Rosen
   March 1986   ISBN 0-88132-020-X

16 The United States and Canada: The Quest for
   Free Trade*   Paul Wonnacott, with an
   appendix by John Williamson
   March 1987   ISBN 0-88132-056-0
17 Adjusting to Success: Balance of Payments
   Policy in the East Asian NICs*
   Bela Balassa and John Williamson
   June 1987, rev. April 1990   ISBN 0-88132-101-X
18 Mobilizing Bank Lending to Debtor
   Countries*   William R. Cline
   June 1987   ISBN 0-88132-062-5
19 Auction Quotas and United States Trade
   Policy*   C. Fred Bergsten, Kimberly Ann
   Elliott, Jeffrey J. Schott, and Wendy E. Takacs
   September 1987   ISBN 0-88132-050-1
20 Agriculture and the GATT: Rewriting the
   Rules*   Dale E. Hathaway
   September 1987   ISBN 0-88132-052-8
21 Anti-Protection: Changing Forces in United
   States Trade Politics*
   I. M. Destler and John S. Odell
   September 1987   ISBN 0-88132-043-9
22 Targets and Indicators: A Blueprint for the
   International Coordination of Economic
   Policy
   John Williamson and Marcus H. Miller
   September 1987   ISBN 0-88132-051-X
23 Capital Flight: The Problem and Policy
   Responses*   Donald R. Lessard and
   John Williamson
   December 1987   ISBN 0-88132-059-5
24 United States-Canada Free Trade: An
   Evaluation of the Agreement*
   Jeffrey J. Schott
   April 1988   ISBN 0-88132-072-2
25 Voluntary Approaches to Debt Relief*
   John Williamson
   Sept. 1988, rev. May 1989   ISBN 0-88132-098-6
26 American Trade Adjustment: The Global
   Impact*   William R. Cline
   March 1989   ISBN 0-88132-095-1
27 More Free Trade Areas?*
   Jeffrey J. Schott
   May 1989   ISBN 0-88132-085-4
28 The Progress of Policy Reform in Latin
   America*   John Williamson
   January 1990   ISBN 0-88132-100-1
29 The Global Trade Negotiations: What Can Be
   Achieved?*   Jeffrey J. Schott
   September 1990   ISBN 0-88132-137-0
30 Economic Policy Coordination: Requiem or
   Prologue?*   Wendy Dobson
   April 1991   ISBN 0-88132-102-8

65 **The Benefits of Price Convergence: Speculative Calculations**
Gary Clyde Hufbauer, Erika Wada, and Tony Warren
December 2001   ISBN 0-88132-333-0

66 **Managed Floating Plus**
Morris Goldstein
March 2002   ISBN 0-88132-336-5

67 **Argentina and the Fund: From Triumph to Tragedy**   Michael Mussa
July 2002   ISBN 0-88132-339-X

68 **East Asian Financial Cooperation**
C. Randall Henning
September 2002   ISBN 0-88132-338-1

69 **Reforming OPIC for the 21st Century**
Theodore H. Moran
May 2003   ISBN 0-88132-342-X

70 **Awakening Monster: The Alien Tort Statute of 1789**
Gary C. Hufbauer and Nicholas Mitrokostas
July 2003   ISBN 0-88132-366-7

71 **Korea after Kim Jong-il**
Marcus Noland
January 2004   ISBN 0-88132-373-X

72 **Roots of Competitiveness: China's Evolving Agriculture Interests**   Daniel H. Rosen, Scott Rozelle, and Jikun Huang
July 2004   ISBN 0-88132-376-4

73 **Prospects for a US-Taiwan FTA**
Nicholas R. Lardy and Daniel H. Rosen
December 2004   ISBN 0-88132-367-5

74 **Anchoring Reform with a US-Egypt Free Trade Agreement**
Ahmed Galal and Robert Z. Lawrence
April 2005   ISBN 0-88132-368-3

75 **Curbing the Boom-Bust Cycle: Stabilizing Capital Flows to Emerging Markets**
John Williamson
July 2005   ISBN 08813-330-6

BOOKS

IMF Conditionality* John Williamson, editor
1983   ISBN 0-88132-006-4

Trade Policy in the 1980s* William R. Cline, ed.
1983   ISBN 0-88132-031-5

Subsidies in International Trade*
Gary Clyde Hufbauer and Joanna Shelton Erb
1984   ISBN 0-88132-004-8

International Debt: Systemic Risk and Policy Response*   William R. Cline
1984   ISBN 0-88132-015-3

Trade Protection in the United States: 31 Case Studies* Gary Clyde Hufbauer, Diane E. Berliner, and Kimberly Ann Elliott
1986   ISBN 0-88132-040-4

Toward Renewed Economic Growth in Latin America* Bela Balassa, Gerardo M. Bueno, Pedro-Pablo Kuczynski, and Mario Henrique Simonsen
1986   ISBN 0-88132-045-5

Capital Flight and Third World Debt*
Donald R. Lessard and John Williamson, editors
1987   ISBN 0-88132-053-6

The Canada-United States Free Trade Agreement: The Global Impact*
Jeffrey J. Schott and Murray G. Smith, editors
1988   ISBN 0-88132-073-0

World Agricultural Trade: Building a Consensus*
William M. Miner and Dale E. Hathaway, editors
1988   ISBN 0-88132-071-3

Japan in the World Economy*
Bela Balassa and Marcus Noland
1988   ISBN 0-88132-041-2

America in the World Economy: A Strategy for the 1990s*   C. Fred Bergsten
1988   ISBN 0-88132-089-7

Managing the Dollar: From the Plaza to the Louvre*   Yoichi Funabashi
1988, 2d. ed. 1989   ISBN 0-88132-097-8

United States External Adjustment and the World Economy*   William R. Cline
May 1989   ISBN 0-88132-048-X

Free Trade Areas and U.S. Trade Policy*
Jeffrey J. Schott, editor
May 1989   ISBN 0-88132-094-3

Dollar Politics: Exchange Rate Policymaking in the United States*
I. M. Destler and C. Randall Henning
September 1989   ISBN 0-88132-079-X

Latin American Adjustment: How Much Has Happened?* John Williamson, editor
April 1990   ISBN 0-88132-125-7

The Future of World Trade in Textiles and Apparel*   William R. Cline
1987, 2d ed. June 1999   ISBN 0-88132-110-9

Completing the Uruguay Round: A Results-Oriented Approach to the GATT Trade Negotiations* Jeffrey J. Schott, editor
September 1990   ISBN 0-88132-130-3

Economic Sanctions Reconsidered (2 volumes)
Economic Sanctions Reconsidered: Supplemental Case Histories
Gary Clyde Hufbauer, Jeffrey J. Schott, and Kimberly Ann Elliott
1985, 2d ed. Dec. 1990   ISBN cloth 0-88132-115-X
ISBN paper 0-88132-105-2

Economic Sanctions Reconsidered: History and Current Policy   Gary Clyde Hufbauer, Jeffrey J. Schott, and Kimberly Ann Elliott
December 1990   ISBN cloth 0-88132-140-0
ISBN paper 0-88132-136-2

Pacific Basin Developing Countries: Prospects for the Future*   Marcus Noland
January 1991   ISBN cloth 0-88132-141-9
ISBN paper 0-88132-081-1

Does Foreign Direct Investment Promote
Development? Theodore Moran, Edward M.
Graham, and Magnus Blomström, editors
April 2005 ISBN 0-88132-381-0
American Trade Politics, 4th ed.
I. M. Destler
June 2005 ISBN 0-88132-382-9

SPECIAL REPORTS

1 Promoting World Recovery: A Statement
on Global Economic Strategy*
by 26 Economists from Fourteen Countries
December 1982 ISBN 0-88132-013-7
2 Prospects for Adjustment in Argentina,
Brazil, and Mexico: Responding to the
Debt Crisis* John Williamson, editor
June 1983 ISBN 0-88132-016-1
3 Inflation and Indexation: Argentina, Brazil,
and Israel* John Williamson, editor
March 1985 ISBN 0-88132-037-4
4 Global Economic Imbalances*
C. Fred Bergsten, editor
March 1986 ISBN 0-88132-042-0
5 African Debt and Financing*
Carol Lancaster and John Williamson, eds.
May 1986 ISBN 0-88132-044-7
6 Resolving the Global Economic Crisis:
After Wall Street*
by Thirty-three Economists from Thirteen
Countries
December 1987 ISBN 0-88132-070-6
7 World Economic Problems*
Kimberly Ann Elliott/John Williamson, editors
April 1988 ISBN 0-88132-055-2
Reforming World Agricultural Trade*
by Twenty-nine Professionals from Seventeen
Countries/1988 ISBN 0-88132-088-9
8 Economic Relations Between the United
States and Korea: Conflict or Cooperation?*
Thomas O. Bayard and Soogil Young, editors
January 1989 ISBN 0-88132-068-4
9 Whither APEC? The Progress to Date and
Agenda for the Future* C. Fred Bergsten, editor
October 1997 ISBN 0-88132-248-2
10 Economic Integration of the Korean
Peninsula Marcus Noland, editor
January 1998 ISBN 0-88132-255-5
11 Restarting Fast Track* Jeffrey J. Schott, editor
April 1998 ISBN 0-88132-259-8
12 Launching New Global Trade Talks:
An Action Agenda Jeffrey J. Schott, editor
September 1998 ISBN 0-88132-266-0

13 Japan's Financial Crisis and Its Parallels to
US Experience
Ryoichi Mikitani and Adam S. Posen, eds.
September 2000 ISBN 0-88132-289-X
14 The Ex-Im Bank in the 21st Century: A New
Approach Gary Clyde Hufbauer
and Rita M. Rodriguez, editors
January 2001 ISBN 0-88132-300-4
15 The Korean Diaspora in the World Economy
C. Fred Bergsten and Inbom Choi, eds.
January 2003 ISBN 0-88132-358-6
16 Dollar Overvaluation and the World
Economy
C. Fred Bergsten and John Williamson, eds.
February 2003 ISBN 0-88132-351-9
17 Dollar Adjustment: How Far? Against What?
C. Fred Bergsten and John Williamson, editors
November 2004 ISBN 0-88132-378-0
18 The Euro at Five: Ready for a Global Role?
Adam S. Posen, editor
April 2005 ISBN 0-88132-380-2

WORKS IN PROGRESS

New Regional Arrangements and
the World Economy
C. Fred Bergsten
The Globalization Backlash in Europe
and the United States
C. Fred Bergsten, Pierre Jacquet, and Karl Kaiser
The United States as a Debtor Nation:
Risks and Policy Reform
William R. Cline
China's Entry into the World Economy
Richard N. Cooper
The ILO in the World Economy
Kimberly Ann Elliott
Reforming Economic Sanctions
Kimberly Ann Elliott, Gary C. Hufbauer,
and Jeffrey J. Schott
Merry Sisterhood or Guarded Watchfulness?
Cooperation Between the IMF and
the World Bank
Michael Fabricius
Why Does Immigration Divide America?
Gordon Hanson
Future of Chinese Exchange Rates
Morris Goldstein and Nicholas R. Lardy
NAFTA Revisited: Achievements
and Challenges
Gary Clyde Hufbauer and Jeffrey J. Schott
The Case for Replacing Corporate Tax Income
Gary Clyde Hufbauer and Paul Greico
New Agricultural Negotiations in the WTO
Tim Josling and Dale Hathaway

**Australia, New Zealand,
and Papua New Guinea**
D.A. Information Services
648 Whitehorse Road
Mitcham, Victoria 3132, Australia
tel: 61-3-9210-7777
fax: 61-3-9210-7788
email: service@adadirect.com.au
www.dadirect.com.au

United Kingdom and Europe
(including Russia and Turkey)
The Eurospan Group
3 Henrietta Street, Covent Garden
London WC2E 8LU England
tel: 44-20-7240-0856
fax: 44-20-7379-0609
www.eurospan.co.uk

Japan and the Republic of Korea
United Publishers Services Ltd.
1-32-5, Higashi-shinagawa,
Shinagawa-ku, Tokyo 140-0002 JAPAN
tel: 81-3-5479-7251
fax: 81-3-5479-7307
info@ups.co.jp
**For trade accounts only.
Individuals will find IIE books in
leading Tokyo bookstores.**

Canada
Renouf Bookstore
5369 Canotek Road, Unit 1
Ottawa, Ontario KlJ 9J3, Canada
tel: 613-745-2665
fax: 613-745-7660
www.renoufbooks.com

India, Bangladesh, Nepal, and Sri Lanka
Viva Books Pvt.
Mr. Vinod Vasishtha
4325/3, Ansari Rd.
Daryaganj, New Delhi-110002
India
tel: 91-11-327-9280
fax: 91-11-326-7224
email: vinod.viva@gndel.globalnet. ems.vsnl.
net.in

Southeast Asia (Brunei, Burma, Cambodia,
Malaysia, Indonesia,
the Philippines, Singapore, Thailand
Taiwan, and Vietnam)
APAC Publishers Services
70 Bedemeer Road #05-03
Hiap Huat House
Singapore 339940
tel: 65-684-47333
fax: 65-674-78916

**Visit our Web site at:
www.iie.com
E-mail orders to:
orders@iie.com**